Ha

Daily Devotionals for Your First Year of
Marriage
By Lynn Miller

BookCaps™ Study Guides

www.bookcaps.com

Cover Image © impuls - Fotolia.com

Table of Contents

Day 1

Today's Scripture Reading: Psalms 37

DEVOTIONAL

This whole chapter is one giant pep talk that you should absolutely apply to your life. It's jam-packed with helpful tidbits! Trust in the Lord, don't worry when evil people appear to be doing well in life, be patient because God has a plan for your life, and so much more! Verses 23-24 are particular encouraging. In short, David says, "No one said you wouldn't fall down. YOU WILL FALL. And it will hurt. But the only way you'll *stay down* is if you refuse to let God help you back up." You see, He will always be there with an outstretched arm waiting to pull you back to your feet. In what ways has the Lord picked you up in the past?

Day 2

Today's Scripture Reading: Proverbs 3:1-4

DEVOTIONAL

For a successful life and a blessed marriage, you should work on memorizing the following two things: Scripture and your wedding vows. The first in that list is a command from the Bible, and the second is a personal suggestion. In the heat of a moment, it can be difficult to see the big picture and remember what's truly noteworthy. Vows oftentimes give an overview of what you want your marriage to look like and the actions you should take in order to ensure that you are headed in the right direction. As for memorizing Scripture, verse after verse in the Bible cites the benefits of doing so.

Day 3

DEVOTIONAL

What does it mean to acknowledge God in all your ways and how can you improve your acknowledgement process as a couple and as individuals? You could try consulting God first and foremost when you are facing a dilemma or celebrating good news. Strive to check in with God first before asking your spouse for advice or calling a friend or family member to share the big news. Consider ceasing to use the word "luck" and focus more on the fact that every good thing in your life is actually a blessing from God. Discuss with your spouse additional ideas that you can implement into your life so you can be known as a couple that acknowledges God in all that you do.

Day 4

Today's Scripture Reading: Proverbs 3:9a

DEVOTIONAL

Possessions can be a stumbling block in your relationship with Christ or a useful tool as you spread His name. Between the two of you, it is likely that you own thousands of different items. How do you honor the Lord with these items? If you are homeowners, are you using your house as a refuge for lost souls? Do you use your blender, electric skillet, and many cooking utensils to cook meals for hungry souls or brothers and sisters in Christ who could use an encouraging meal? Take the time right now to make a list of five things you can do within the next week to honor the Lord with your possessions.

Day 5

Today's Scripture Reading: Proverbs 9b:-10

DEVOTIONAL

Which is a more accurate description of your giving to God; "off the top" or "random leftovers?" Scripture says time and time again that we should give our "firstfruits" to God, but what exactly does that mean? It might mean setting aside your contribution before you participate in any shopping trips or date nights. Maybe it means that you give the first part of your day (and your time) to God by communing with Him in prayer or reading Scripture. One thing is for sure, though--the Creator of the universe deserves far more than your leftovers. How will you sacrifice to Him first this week?

Day 6

Today's Scripture Reading: Proverbs 3:21-26

DEVOTIONAL

When your head hits the pillow at night, do you occasionally struggle with silencing the worldly concerns that swirl round and round in your head? With cancer, global warming, road fatalities, stock market instability, and identity theft, we certainly have a lot to worry about these days. According to Solomon, there is actually a way that we can sleep easy at night, feeling the presence of God at our side and fearing no disaster. He indicates that wisdom, understanding, sound judgment, and discretion are the secret fear-busters of society. Exercise these values and you might just catch some better Zzzzs!

Day 7

DEVOTIONAL

We can receive discipline and correction from God in many different ways. Sometimes it's as simple as receiving a natural consequence for a decision you made. Other times, His correction can take a less direct approach. Maybe a friend or family member has called you out before when you have been acting less than Christ-like. Or perhaps your heart and conscience were struck by a message you heard from the pulpit. It can be uncomfortable to be corrected, but consider it a compliment from God. He wants us to be the best that we can be! This is why He will occasionally use our loved ones to refine us into the mature and holy children that we are called to be. Discuss how God has used someone to correct you in the past. How might you and your spouse work to improve your attitudes when accepting God's discipline and correction?

Day 8

Today's Scripture Reading: Proverbs 4:14-19

DEVOTIONAL

There are some paths of evil in the world today that can be quite enticing, or fascinating at the very least. We might be tempted to exercise the mindset of a parent speaking to a child in a crystal shop, "You can look, but don't touch." Well, we all know that letting a child loose inside a room full of breakables will likely result in chaos and a fair amount of damage. The Bible doesn't take the look-but-don't-touch stance when it comes to sin. Solomon tells us here that when you see some sinful temptation, you should look away, turn around, and *avoid* that path with everything you have inside you. Many a good-intentioned soul has fallen prey to sin because they chose to walk on by and check out the scenery, instead of taking the long way around.

Day 9

Today's Scripture Reading: Proverbs 4:20-27

DEVOTIONAL

Here, Solomon tells us that we should protect our hearts. In doing so, we will undoubtedly positively influence the "issues of life" that spring forth from it. He indicates that, in order to protect our hearts, we should do the following three things:

*Keep the words (AKA *these* Scriptures) in our hearts,

*Avoid those who speak in a deceitful and/or perverse manner, and

*Always be searching for and focusing on the path of righteousness.

Do the words of the Bible resonate in your hearts? Is there a co-worker, friend, or television show in your lives right now that speaks in the negative manner that Solomon describes in these verses? Finally, do you sometimes find yourselves being overly interested in or tempted by the sinful lifestyles of those around you?

Day 10

Today's Scripture Reading: Proverbs 5:1-23

DEVOTIONAL

This entire chapter can be summed up in two words and five exclamation points: DON'T CHEAT!!!!!! Solomon dedicates this entire chapter to the concept, as well Proverbs 6:24-29 and 7:1-27. Although this warning is written to a son, you could easily replace the gender-specific language to reflect a letter written to a daughter. The overall message of these three passages is this—an adulterous relationship *will destroy you.* Consider the image that he has painted with his words. The NKJV says that an adulterer will be "on the verge of total ruin (5:14)...reduced to a crust of bread (6:26)." Solomon also goes into extensive description regarding how appealing an adulterous woman can appear to be. Be frank with one another. In the future, what might be tempting about participating in an extramarital relationship? Now, what is the *reality* of adultery? Who do you know who has experienced the repercussions of that decision firsthand and how did it affect their life?

Day 11

Today's Scripture Reading: Proverbs 6:6-11

DEVOTIONAL

While we don't live in the agricultural-centered society that once existed, the concept of saving our harvest for harder times is still a dominant theme. In Bible times, they used to set aside a portion of their summer harvest so they would have food to eat in the winter. Nowadays we set aside money (in the form of 401k and/or IRA accounts) so that we will be taken care of in the future. Consider the following questions with your spouse:

*What issues can arise if you sleep when you should be working (verse 9-10)?

*What issues can arise if you *only* think of the future and what it may hold?

*What are some practical ways that you can balance those two extremes?

Today's Scripture Reading: Proverbs 6:12-19

Ah, things the Lord hates. We read about murder and constantly devising evil plans and running down evil paths and think, "No way. That doesn't describe me." Sometimes we skip over the more common (but equally detested by God) sins that trip us up a bit more than the rest. How about that proud look or lying tongue? God HATES them! They rank right up there with murder in His opinion. Since He'll be judging at the end of time and not us, I would say that His is the *only* opinion that matters. For today, consider why God finds "a proud look" an abomination to Him and discuss how you can avoid displeasing God in this manner.

58.) Today's Scripture Reading: Proverbs 10:12

Some think the idea that all anyone needs is love originated with a popular British band in the 1960's, but we see in this brief verse that the Bible had that concept pinned down a long time ago! There's no doubt that hatred can stir up MANY unfortunate and complicated situations, but how can falling back on love help you look past the sins of your spouse? Here's a helpful tip: When you're angry at your spouse and everything inside of you is telling you to give the silent treatment, make yourself hold hands with your spouse or place your hand on his or her arm. This loving physical gesture may jumpstart your mind into thinking lovingly, as well. What other ways can you call up love in a moment of anger?

Day 12

Today's Scripture Reading: Proverbs 10:8,10,14,19 and Proverbs 18:13

DEVOTIONAL

Proverbs is chock-full of admonitions about the dangers of running your mouth. Life gets exciting, and it can be easy to "chatter" (as the NIV puts it), but there is terrific value in taking time to listen to others instead of filling the world with senseless small talk. Think back to a time when you missed an important piece of information or a lesson because you were preoccupied with making sure that your opinion was heard. It's easy to get distracted and tune out a speaker. Sometimes, before they've even finished their sentence, you're already planning what you're going to say when they stop talking. It happens frequently, but it shouldn't. As you go to work, sit in church, and interact with your spouse, make a concerted effort to listen fully. If you truly listen, you might just learn something you desperately need to know.

Day 13

Today's Scripture Reading: Proverbs 11:1

DEVOTIONAL

In Bible times, dishonest scales were used to rip off a customer. A vendor might rest the weight of his hand on a scale while weighing out a customer's barley, potentially resulting in the customer paying for 2 pounds of goods when he only received 1 ½ pounds! It sounds despicable and utterly dishonest, but dishonest work practices are still used today and they have expanded far beyond scale scandals. Have you ever known a co-worker who has advanced in his or her profession using dishonest measures and tricks? If you constantly work hard continually find yourself a step behind others using less honest approaches, you might be tempted to cut corners. Fight that temptation! The Bible doesn't say that the dishonest will never prosper on earth, but it does say that the Lord gains pleasure from your diligent efforts. His opinion of you is worth far more than any promotion you could ever obtain.

Day 14

DEVOTIONALS

We've all met two-face people, or sometimes even three- and four-faced ones! How about the woman who talks a righteous talk on Sunday mornings, but revels in sin on Friday night? Or the man who exudes the values of strong Christian leadership in his family, but can be seen frequenting the sketchy late-night joints around town. There are less extreme examples of duplicity, as well. It's natural to adjust your manner of speaking and acting depending on your company. You probably wouldn't show the goofiest side of your personality to your boss on your first day of work, but you wouldn't hesitate to loosen up and let your crazy flag fly free when you're with your family. In the sense of this scripture, do you think there is a discrepancy in how you speak and act around different groups of people? What negative forms of duplicity should you address in your life?

Day 15

DEVOTIONALS

The people of Solomon's time desperately yearned to have mortal men leading them. God gave His people the gift of living without a king and what did they do? They BEGGED Him to anoint a king to rule over them! Unbelievable, yet we're still hanging our hopes on mortal men today. Whether it's the pastor of your church, the President of the United States, or the Chief Executive Officer who signs your paycheck, we see that mortal men can make a temporary difference in the world, but the only lasting difference was made by our one true king, Jesus Christ of Nazareth. Who are the mortals you've been placing your hopes in? One culprit might even be your spouse. Discuss the complications that can arise from trusting in man more than trusting in God.

Day 16

DEVOTIONALS

In today's society, is there anything juicier than a fresh secret? Our ears perk up once we hear, "Ok, you can't tell anyone else this, but you'll never guess what I just heard!" In all that we do, however, we should strive to be trustworthy people. Would your friends describe you as a fortified steel vault or a loose-lipped confidant? In what ways can you avoid the treacherous waters of gossip and strengthen your trustworthiness? Perhaps you and your spouse have a no-secrets policy. While this is fine, and possibly even GREAT, it's important that your friends know that you exercise full honesty with your spouse. If they realize that confiding in you is equal to confiding in your spouse, they will be able to make an informed decision about which things they would like to share and which things they'd rather keep hush-hush.

Day 17

Today's Scripture Reading: Proverbs 12:4

DEVOTIONAL

A crown is associated with status, wealth, power, and class. If you see someone wearing a crown (and we're not talking about a Burger King crown or a dress-up tiara), that person would stand out from all the others around you as peculiar. What a blessing that WIVES can grant their husbands with an elevated status simply by being noble. The term "noble" is not one that is frequently used in our culture, so look it up in a dictionary if you're not certain what it means. Then you can talk about what the act of being noble could look like. Wives, ask your husbands what you could do to increase your noble-factor. Husbands, thank your wives for all the things they do, big and small, that promotes nobility in your lives.

Day 18

Today's Scripture Reading: Proverbs 12:8, 16:22-23, and 19:14

DEVOTIONAL

Now, prudence is a truly antiquated word these days. In a nutshell, prudence means that you are able to control your life by using reason. It requires being disciplined. It requires some knowledge and logic in order to even know *how* to use reason in your life. A "warped mind" (NIV) is something that we all know a little too much about, though. With school shootings, record-high occurrences of rape and abuse, and about 40 prime-time television shows about creepy serial killers, we all know what a warped mind looks like. It's probably pretty safe to say that people wouldn't describe you as having a warped mind, but could they see proof of prudence in your life? If so, what are some specific examples that you have shown recently?

Day 19

DEVOTIONAL

Even though Americans are among some of the richest individuals in the world, there seems to be an epidemic of always needing, seeking, and wanting more. It seems to be one giant game of Keep-Up-With-The-Jones' where everyone loses. Instead of comparing ourselves to others who have less than we do, we compare ourselves to the richest and most privileged people in our communities. There's always a better car, better house, and better job on the horizon. Some of the (seemingly) richest people have been forced into bankruptcy, though. Years of pretending to have more than they actually did landed them even deeper in debt than the average bottom-dweller. So, the next time you compare yourself to the Jones', consider the blessings you have and realize that some of what you're seeing might just be a facade.

Day 20

*Today's Scripture Reading: Proverbs 12:15 and
15:22*

DEVOTIONAL

We live in a culture that encourages individualism
and independent thought almost to a fault. The two
phrases "Better to ask for forgiveness later than to ask
for permission now," and "Too many cooks in the
kitchen spoil the broth," indicate that we would rather
not include others in our decision-making process. In
these two scriptures, Solomon is saying to us, "Hey, I
know you think you're on the right path, but if you'd
ask around a bit, you'd find that there's a much better
way to accomplish your goals." Hopefully you will
always include your spouse in your decision-making
process. Who is someone else who has proven to be a
wise advisor to you and how has their advice helped
divert you from failing in the past?

Day 21

DEVOTIONAL

Society glorifies the idea of following your instincts, which oftentimes involves speaking thoughts the moment they cross your mind. Unfortunately, exercising this form of free expression in your marriage can cause serious damage. Have you ever wondered why they call it a "gut instinct?" Maybe because it can cause gut-wrenching pain? Or maybe because guts are ugly and sometimes the truth is, too! The Bible tells us that rash words are like weapons of destruction. Keep this in mind as you strive to be truthful and loving to your spouse. When in doubt, wait a beat. A few minutes of reflection can make all the difference between words that wound and words that heal.

Day 22

Today's Scripture Reading: Proverbs 12:25

DEVOTIONAL

In this ever-changing world in which we live, there are many things that can cause us to be anxious. Try to remember a time in your life when you felt consumed with anxiety. What thoughts helped you see through the worries and gain a more positive perspective? Share your answer with your spouse. Now, when you see that your mate is plagued by doubt you can speak those "kind words" to lighten the burden your loved one is carrying. Additionally, you might consider writing a handwritten note or sending a sincere e-mail or text message to someone you know who is struggling with anxiety.

Day 23

Today's Scripture Reading: Proverbs 13:20

DEVOTIONAL

With whom do you walk with on a daily basis? Take a mental inventory of the company you keep at work and in your leisure time. Think about which of your friends bombard you with post after post on social media sites and what the content of those posts are like. Are you surrounded by foolish or wise companions? If you're hanging out with men and women filled with wisdom--you're in luck! Their wisdom will rub off on you. However, it's bad news if your friends are fools, because they will rub off on you, too. Are there any companions that are influencing your lives poorly? Consider reducing the amount of time you spend with them and you might just notice a difference.

Day 24

Today's Scripture Reading: Proverbs 15:1 and 18

DEVOTIONAL

As a newly married couple, you can expect to engage in your fair share of arguments. What can keep an argument from turning into a full blown fight is the way in which you respond to your loved one's elevated level of anger and frustration. Each time one of you has a temper that's flaring, the other one has a tremendous opportunity to show love and diffuse the situation OR to throw fuel on the fire and get ready for a yelling match. What's it gonna be? A gentle answer or a harsh word? Count to five before you answer, take a deep breath, and repeat this verse in your head if you want to be a peacemaker in your relationship.

Day 25

DEVOTIONAL

The Lord is pleased by your prayers. Isn't that a lovely thought? A prayer doesn't cost you a thing, is not physically taxing, and can occur at any time of the day in absolutely any location. How often are you pleasing the Lord by offering your prayers up to Him? Is it only before meals or just before you go to sleep? Are you praying as a couple and individually, as well? Please the Lord by offering him a heartfelt prayer right now. Empty your soul to Him as freely as you would to your spouse. Feel free to pray together at this time. If you don't know where to start, consider alternating telling God one thing for which you are thankful and one thing with which you need His help.

Day 26

DEVOTIONAL

If you've got your nose up in the air, you'll never see the holes, sticks, curbs, and speed bumps in life that will trip you up. Pride! It's an ongoing struggle for many people in our society and of what exactly do we have to be proud? All blessings come from God. That includes our successes and possessions. Our skills come from Him, too, so we can't brag on those either. Are there any areas in your life where you are struggling with prideful thoughts? If so, take heed; a fall may be in your near future. If you note that your spouse it getting a little too self-confident, gently help him or her remember that all blessings come from God. If you strive to give Him the glory and not yourselves, you won't be disappointed.

Day 27

DEVOTIONAL

Throughout your time together, you will periodically be faced with big decisions that will alter your lives significantly. You may have to choose where to live, what job to take, when to have kids, and how you will discipline them. There will be many more decisions, too—ranging from picking which political candidate you will support to how you will invest your hard-earned money. While you should always strive to make good choices, you can rest assured knowing that God's plan and purpose will ultimately prevail. Think about a decision that you will have to make in the near future. Weigh two different outcomes and imagine how God could use either choice to serve His purpose in the future. The possibilities are endless!

Day 28

Today's Scripture Reading: Proverbs 17:14

DEVOTIONAL

This verse is the epitome of the age-old advice, "Choose your battles." It's amazing how once a quarrel gets started there seems to be no going back. You can't take back the things you say in the heat of moment, nor can you take back your actions. As the verse says, it's like breaking open a dam. Once the damage is done, things won't slow down enough for you to repair the situation in an adequate fashion. If you have had a dam break in your lives lately, you know the truth of this statement. No need to rehash a past quarrel, but it may be wise to consider the repercussions before you participate in another.

Day 29

Today's Scripture Reading: Proverbs 17:17

DEVOTIONAL

Now that you are married, it is of the utmost importance that you stand by each other's sides through times of adversity. Much of your life together will be filled with pleasant times and easy sailing, but it is the times of adversity that will define you. You will also do the Lord proud when you, as a couple, support your friends as they face trials. It's always a blessing to have a friend you can call no matter what who will always be willing to pick you up in the middle of the night when you're stranded. Someone you can call to cry and vent to and someone who will loan you money, a couch to sleep on, or a ride to the airport. Continually work to be that friend to each other and to those around you.

Day 30

DEVOTIONAL

Have you ever seen a movie where a giant tornado terrorized a town? Or maybe you've watched actual news coverage of one of the many hurricanes that have ravaged various coastal cities around the world. When a storm is brewing, people run to their basements, storm shelters, or maybe even get out of town completely! Where do you flee to ensure your safety? It's a powerful thought to consider. In Bible times, a fortified tower would be that place. When enemies would attack and seek to plunder a town, you wanted to be in that fortified tower and would do whatever it took to get there! In times of physical, mental, and emotional danger, where would you run? As you evaluate your plans for safety, make sure God is at the center of all of them. Include prayer on your emergency checklist and call on His name whenever you feel that your safety may be jeopardized.

Day 31

Today's Scripture Reading: Proverbs 18:17

DEVOTIONAL

Every time you make a decision, you should want it to be an informed one. It's kind of like shopping around. Let's say you're looking for a new car. If the salesman just showed you one car and only listed that car's specifications, mileage, and safety features that car might sound pretty good to you. But you would be foolish not to consider what other salesmen and other cars had to offer. When it comes to believing a person's word, it becomes even more beneficial to get the facts about the whole situation. It's easy to believe one person's side of the story if you never hear from the second party. The next time you (or your spouse) are spouting off your point of view about a situation, question what the *other* person's story is and make your decision accordingly, but only once you have the whole story.

Day 32

Today's Scripture Reading: Proverbs 18:22 and Genesis 2:18-24

DEVOTIONAL

To the husbands:

You found a wife! Congratulations! You can go ahead and check that box. What a beautiful realization it is to know that by marrying your wife you not only gained a valuable helper, but also received the favor of the Lord. The partnership that you and your wife share was designed by God in the very beginning of time. He ordained your marriage, and you please Him by honoring, respecting, and cherishing your wife and the bond that you two have together. In a society where marriage slowly moves lower and lower down the list of priorities, you should know that God supports your marriage just as strongly as He supported Adam and Eve's in the beginning. Tell your wife you love her, give her a kiss, and smile up at God because He is certainly smiling down on you as He sends good favor your way.

Day 33

Today's Scripture Reading: Proverbs 19:13 and 21:9, 19

DEVOTIONAL

Solomon mentions the downfalls of having a "quarrelsome" and "nagging" wife multiple times throughout the book of Proverbs. Men, since you have already chosen your wives, your control of this situation is over. The women, however, can work on harnessing these potentially negative character traits in order to ensure that your husbands are not wishing they were in a desert instead of living under the same roof with you! "Nagging" is such a strong word. Perhaps you can identify more with the idea of incessantly reminding your husband about something of which he is already aware. When you feel yourself staring to nag or start a fight, ask yourself the following three questions:

1.) What will be gained if I continue on this course?

2.) What is the worst thing that could happen if I *don't* say what I'm thinking right now?

3.) If I *do* say what I'm thinking, what kind of reaction will this elicit from my husband and what kind of admonish might I receive from God? ("Well done" or "Be patient," for example.)

Day 34

Today's Scripture Reading: Proverbs 21:13 and 22:9

DEVOTIONAL

Step 1.) Right now, as a couple, identify who the "poor" are in your lives.

Step 2.) Discuss what it is that these poor people need. What have they asked for in the past? What are needs that *you* see, but they don't verbalize?

Step 3.) Meet their needs.

It's a simple concept. If you can't think of any poor, then you probably haven't been looking hard enough. We live in a world that is simply NOT FAIR. Some are born into poverty and some into wealth. Not only can you share the love of Christ as you meet the needs of others, but you will please God and also ensure that your needs will be taken care of when you are in distress.

Day 35

Today's Scripture Reading: Proverbs 22:1

DEVOTIONAL

Money can buy a whole lot of things in this world, but one of the things it cannot buy is a good name. Your reputation is one of the most valuable assets you have, even though it has no monetary worth on its own. Take your spouse, for example. Before you began a dating relationship with your spouse, did you consider what his or her reputation was like? Chances are if your spouse had a reputation of lying, cheating, breaking hearts, deceiving others and being lazy you might not have ended up getting hitched! What would the world say is your collective (as a couple) reputation and what can you do to further improve your "good name?"

Day 36

Today's Scripture Reading: Proverbs 22:6

DEVOTIONAL

Perhaps the pitter-patter of little baby feet are already ringing through your hallways, or maybe you two are waiting until you get a little farther down the road before you start popping out those lil' bundles of joy. If child-bearing is in your future, it would be wise to begin discussing the way in which you will parent your children before you see those two pink lines on the pregnancy test. As you read about and see examples of different parenting styles around you, make an effort to deliberate the pros and cons of those different strategies. Feel free to talk about how *you* were raised as a child and which methods you feel strongly about continuing to enforce. So long as your parenting methods are consistent with raising your child up in the ways of the Lord, you will be a success!

Day 37

DEVOTIONAL

Although Solomon frequently mentions the importance of working and not being lazy, he bluntly tells us that it is not a worthwhile aspiration to become rich. Don't wear yourselves out stashing away paycheck after paycheck in hopes of leading a comfortable life! You could waste away your whole life storing up monetary blessings for yourselves and they could be gone in the blink of an eye. Theft, a substantial stock market crash, unexpected crises, death, or the triumphal return of Jesus Christ could well occur during your time on this Earth. Being rich won't amount to a hill of beans in any of the aforementioned situations. Take a mental inventory of how you've been spending your allotted time thus far. Are you pushing 60-hour weeks at the office? Consider the cost and the benefits of your money-related decisions, all the while keeping in mind that the only "rich" people in God's mind are rich in Spirit.

Day 38

DEVOTIONAL

Are you familiar with the concept that too much of a good thing can be a bad thing? Everything in moderation. The problem is that society has forgotten what moderation even looks like! With a "Carpe Diem" attitude, not giving a care for consequences, people seek to experience all that they can, as fast as they can, as often as they can. While God gave us many pleasant things that we can enjoy, He did not intend for us to gorge ourselves on them. Too much food results in health problems such as obesity, heart disease, and diabetes. Too much screen time can interfere with our social interactions and overall productivity. Think about something in your life that is good that you may benefit from cutting back a bit. If there's nothing you can bring to mind at this exact moment—great! But don't forget to think about this question going forward from here.

Day 39

DEVOTIONAL

Here's an intriguing verse for you. When you read this passage, what does it make you think about in today's language? How about sarcasm or practical jokes? While joking is mostly only meant for good-natured fun, there are some people who use it to rile up their friends and neighbors or to make them look like fools. Sarcasm, like any other words from your mouth, can be used to wound and insult others. If sarcasm is a daily part of your repertoire, you may not need to cut it out altogether. You may just need to identify individuals who might be most prone to misconstruing your true intentions and meaning.

Day 40

Today's Scripture Reading: Proverbs 27:2

DEVOTIONAL

Our culture is one filled with shameless amounts of self-promotion. We pat ourselves on the back in the content we post on social media, beef our resumes up with every positive thing we can think to say about ourselves, and are quick to fish for compliments when we feel that we are due them. That's not how Scripture suggests we conduct ourselves, though. It's an act of humility when you are able to "deserve" praise, but not require it. While it is human nature to crave validation for our efforts, we need to be content with doing a terrific job for the sake of quality and not attention. But if your spouse is avoiding complimenting him- or herself, feel free to shower him or her with compliments. In doing so, one of you will exercise love while the other gets an opportunity to tackle humility.

Day 41

DEVOTIONAL

How you say something can be much more valuable that *what* you're saying. Tone and nonverbals play a HUGE role in communication. You more than likely know this already since you are married. It's an all-too-common scenario when a husband asks his wife if she's mad and she crosses her arms, looks out the window and says, "I'm fine." Or how about when the wife asks her husband if he's listening and he answers, "Yes," in a mono-toned voice, all while never looking away from his video game. In all interactions with your spouse, aim to speak loving words, *in a loving way*, with all sincerity.

Day 42

Today's Scripture Reading: Proverbs 27:17

DEVOTIONAL

Iron--such a strong and seemingly indestructible substance--requires improvement from time to time. It takes an equally strong substance to sharpen it, which is quite interesting. Even Christians who seem entirely confident in their faith, committed to the Lord, and unwavering in their dedication need to be sharpened by other Christians periodically. In your marriage, do you find that your faith, zeal, and knowledge of God's message grows stronger when you study and worship with your spouse? Discuss ways in which you can better sharpen each other and take this week to implement as least one of the ideas that you brainstorm.

Day 43

Today's Scripture Reading: Proverbs 28:13

DEVOTIONAL

We've all done things that we're not proud of doing.
Sometimes we may even be so ashamed of our
actions or thoughts that we hide the truth from others
around us. It's important that we not attempt to hide
these things from God, though. Sure, deep down
inside we may know that it's pointless to try and hide
anything from an all-knowing deity, but for some
reason (Comfort? Fear? Habit?) we try to do it
anyway. The same is true when it comes to our
spouses. Try as you might to be honest with your
spouse, there may still be some buried secrets you
would benefit from releasing. If you can think of
anything that has been bothering you, confess to God
and your spouse. I promise you'll feel better, and this
passage even goes so far as to say that you will
prosper for it.

Day 44

Today's Scripture Reading: Proverbs 31:4-7

DEVOTIONAL

If it's not a terrific idea for kings and princes to get drunk, it might not be so great for you to do, either. Solomon suggested that alcohol could inhibit an individual's ability to decipher right from wrong, consequently resulting in misconstruing the rules and breaking the law. Additionally, he suggests that we should leave drunkenness for those who are low and dying so they can temporarily escape from their misery. Regardless of whether or not you agree with Solomon's admonition, you should make sure that you're on the same page with your spouse regarding the role of alcoholic beverages in your life.

Day 45

Today's Scripture Reading: Proverbs 31:10-31

DEVOTIONAL

Wives, I don't blame you if you read these verses and think, "Man! That is a tall order to fill." Honestly, it is. In short, this ideal wife is running herself ragged caring for the needs of her household. She's an entrepreneur, a chef, a manager, a philanthropist, a seamstress, an early riser, and an overall gem in the rough. So, you're new the wife business. It may take you years to aspire to this level of multi-tasking, but at least this example gives you something to aspire to. Overall, this wife is simply a hard worker, a household planner, and a lover of her family. If you can manage to nail down those three attributes, I'd say you might be worth far more than rubies, as well!

Day 46

Today's Scripture Reading: Jeremiah 15:16

DEVOTIONAL

There's just something about sharing a meal that brings people together. Think of the most memorable meal that you have ever shared with your spouse. Was it romantic? Maybe it was unique or exotic in some way. Or maybe it was a big family meal with all the fixings. Whatever it was, I doubt it was as filling as the meal Jeremiah refers to in Jeremiah 15:16. One of the best things you can do with your spouse is to feast on the Word together. Do this on a daily basis and blessings will abound! Reading this book is a superb start. Continue to delve deeper and deeper into the Scriptures and I promise that you will grow closer as you learn and grow together.

Day 47

Today's Scripture Reading: Matthew 5:17-20

DEVOTIONAL

What do you think about when you hear the word *commandments*? If you are like most people, you think of Moses climbing Mount Sinai and bringing ten specific rules down to the Israelites. Those are certainly the most famous commandments, but really, a commandment could be any mandate, direct order, or specific instruction. Today's Bible reading indicates that we should not set aside even the *least* of the commandments. If we do, we are teaching others (our mate, our friends, our co-workers) that A.) we can pick and choose what we like from Scripture and B.) they need not obey certain commandments since we aren't obeying them. As you read through the Bible with your spouse, make a note of each direct instruction (AKA "commandment") you come across and ask each other, "Are we fulfilling this order to the best of our ability, or have we mistakenly skipped over it?"

Day 48

Today's Scripture Reading: Matthew 5:27-30

DEVOTIONAL

What a tough scripture! And take note, this applies to men *and* women. Satan has made it increasing difficult to control our roaming eyes by feeding society lies about what is fashionable and what is appropriate. All you have to do is go to the grocery store checkout line to see a woman in front of you wearing an obscenely tight shirt, cleavage galore on the magazine covers, and long legs with barely-there short skirts around every corner. We can't control what others around us wear, but we can control A.) how long our eyes linger, B.) which thoughts we dwell on, and C.) what we choose to view in the comfort of our own homes. Rid your magazine stash, internet browser, movie collection, and DVR playlist of any potentially lustful stumbling blocks. Commit to each other here and now that you will advocate purity in your house and in your mind.

Day 49

Today's Scripture Reading: Matthew 5:31-32

DEVOTIONAL

As newlyweds, I hope this stage of your marriage is simple, exciting, and joyous. You are learning to navigate the world together, and there are so many possibilities before you. However, there are many seasons of marriage and you may find yourselves going through some pretty tremendous storms in your future together. Satan has a vast supply of different attacks he will try to throw at you. The Bible is clear on the topic of divorce, though. Jesus Himself says that there is one, and only one, legitimate reason for it. Therefore, no matter how bad your knock-down, drag-out fight is, leave the "D" word out of it. Abandoning ship is not an option. If you sail into your storms devoted to that line of thinking, it probably won't make the fallout any more pleasant. However, at least when the waves subside both of your compasses will be pointing in the right direction.

Day 50

Today's Scripture Reading: Matthew 5:43-48

<u>DEVOTIONAL</u>

We all know the Bible says time and time again that we should love our enemies. I can't remember the last time I heard anyone tell me, "Oh, no. I don't hang out with so-and-so. She's my ENEMY!" Batman and Wonder Woman have enemies; we have people who are just not our favorites or not on our side. Sometimes our enemies only last for a day and other times they are a daily pain in your side. Maybe you're not crazy about your co-worker who shirks his responsibilities at work which causes you to have to pick up his slack. Or maybe you accidentally overheard your friend at church complaining about how you teach his or her child in your weekly Sunday school class. Whether your daily "enemies" are constant complainers, consistent procrastinators, or steady stuck-ups, they need your love. Tell your spouse about two people who have made it difficult for you to have a good day recently and pray for those individuals right now. If you start showing these difficult people love in your prayer life now, that attitude might just work its way into your daily interactions later.

Day 51

Today's Scripture Reading: Matthew 6:1-4

DEVOTIONAL

While this Scripture can certainly apply to your interactions with others throughout your life, it can also *definitely* apply to random or not-so-random acts of kindness that you do for your spouse. The sweetest of gifts are anonymous and never require or expect repayment. You needn't bring attention to every kind thing you do for your mate. Love him or her fully and you will automatically put his or her happiness first in big and small matters. So what if you burned one of the pork chops? You take the toasty one and leave it at that. Maybe you could sit down behind the lady with big hair at the concert so that the love of your life doesn't have to deal with such a distraction. No need to toot your own horn—the happiness of your mate should be sufficient.

Day 52

Today's Scripture Reading: Matthew 6:16-17

DEVOTIONAL

Our Savior does not say, "*If* you fast," but He does says, "*When* you fast." Coincidence? I think not. Fasting is a long forgotten form of spiritual devotion, but it is one that can richly bless your life and bring you closer to God and more in touch with the Holy Spirit. Fasting is, of course, much easier if the people around you aren't stuffing their faces and sending delicious smelling aromas in your direction as you attempt to pray and mediate on the Scriptures. I challenge the two of you to purposefully abstain from eating one meal together tomorrow. Use the time you would have been eating to read the Bible together. Once you've conquered that challenge, I would suggest that you fast for an entire day sometime within the next two weeks. Each time your stomach growls or you feel a pang of temptation to grab that snack cake and cheat, pray. Thank the Lord for the sustenance that He provides on a daily basis and ask that you would hunger for Him and for spiritual food just as you hunger for physical food. Don't forget to share your thoughts on your fasting experience with your spouse. Who knows? You may even decide to make fasting a regular part of your worship to God.

Day 53

Today's Scripture Reading: Matthew 7:1-6

DEVOTIONAL

Marriage is a fantastic, WONDERFUL union that is *so* worth waiting for. In fact, it's so fabulous that we oftentimes hold our spouses to unobtainable expectations. Think about the most recent thing that you got on your spouse's back about. He doesn't do enough sweet things to show that he loves you? She talks too much and doesn't ask your opinion? Maybe you're both wishing for a little more R-E-S-P-E-C-T? Stop and ponder for a moment if it's possible that your spouse is not the only one at fault in this predicament. Before you pick, pick, pick at what your mate could being doing better, prayerfully question what *you* could be doing to be a better spouse. Don't be surprised if you pull the equivalent of a small lumberyard out of your eye before you get to your silver anniversary.

Day 54

Today's Scripture Reading: Matthew 7:7-12

DEVOTIONAL

Hopefully the channels of communication are wide open between you and your spouse. Perhaps you tell each other how your day has been or what your hopes, dreams, fears, and goals are. It's easy to tell our spouses what we are thinking, feeling, and wanting because A.) it is expected of us, and B.) we know our spouses want to give us the desires of our hearts, and C.) we anticipate a response from them. These three things are true of God, too. God expects you to communicate your desires with Him and He *wants* bless you with what you want. Next time you hear your spouse wishing he or she could get that promotion at work or gain some self-confidence that has been lacking, ask if he or she has brought that request to God. Offer to pray with your spouse as you ask, seek, and knock together.

Day 55

Today's Scripture Reading: Matthew 8:18-22

DEVOTIONAL

If you're reading these devotionals, it's a pretty safe bet that you desire a relationship with Christ, and you want to follow Him daily. That's a great start! Life gets in the way, though. You might be tempted to think, "I'll really devote more of my time to church activities once I have kids," or "I'll go on more mission trips once I retire." Maybe you feel like you need to reach a certain level of success in your career and have stable finances before you truly follow Him with reckless abandon. While tempting, those aren't adequate excuses for our Lord and Savior. He requires that you follow Him NOW, even when it means you might miss out on something in the meantime. What is holding you back today?

Day 56

DEVOTIONAL

Church has gotten a bad rap for being more like a country club than a hospital. Many hold the belief that church is where people who have it all together go and to dress up and learn about how they can keep it together. This is occasionally true—probably more often than it should be. We need to be reaching out to the sick. Do a mental inventory of the kinds of people with which you and your spouse associate. Do they all look, act, dress, and talk just like you? Or maybe you are already reaching out to those who are different, looked down upon by society, and sick. It is these people who don't know the love of Christ, and you might just be the one person who is supposed to look past their ailments and administer the cure. You have an unlimited supply of the vaccination, which is the Good News. Are you willing to mingle with the diseased in order to distribute it?

Day 57

Today's Scripture Reading: Matthew 9:35-38

DEVOTIONAL

Do you ever wonder who the Lord intends for you to share the Gospel with? Maybe you're looking around and saying, "These people don't seem interested in the news I have to share," or "All my friends are already saved." The fact of the matter is that there are MANY whose hearts and lives are in the perfect place to hear about the Lord and accept Him as their Savior. You must find them, though! When it comes to harvesting, have you ever heard about carts and bushels of grain and produce magically appearing in a farmer's barn? No! Workers must be sent out to collect the ripe foods, just like Christ sends us out to minister to ready hearts. Pray together right now and ask that the Lord would lead you to whomever needs to hear the Good News. Don't worry if a person doesn't come to Jesus immediately. Even ripe produce that is ready for harvest may sometimes have a deep root system that you must break up before you can wrestle the prize free.

Day 58

DEVOTIONAL

This passage is a tough one to swallow. Anytime you receive notice that you are soon to be HATED by many, it's not a great day. If someone already has a negative disposition toward you, it can be increasing difficult for that person to accept anything you say. Take heart. Matthew is essentially saying, "Don't worry. You can't say the right things to these 'haters.' You can't, but God can. And the Spirit will speak through your lips without you even having to give it a second thought." Wow! How amazing! You can be bad with words (like Moses said/thought he was) and still eloquently state the case for Christ. Tell your spouse about a time in your life (if you can think of one) when the Spirit seemed to speak through you? How does knowing that the Lord can speak through your lips change your outlook on speaking to strangers about your relationship with Christ?

Day 59

Today's Scripture Reading: Matthew 12:46-50

DEVOTIONAL

Maybe you've heard the saying, "Blood is thicker than water." It's a common societal value to pledge ultimate allegiance to one's family, but Jesus overturned that tradition in the same manner in which he challenged many others. Fellow believers *are* your family now. Think about the unwritten rules that apply to your mom, big brothers, and/or little sisters. You may try to assume the best about them before you jump to conclusions thinking the worst, avoid disgracing yourself because you know it would reflect poorly on them, and/or might kid around with them from time to time, but allow no one else to make fun of them. What if we treated our spiritual brothers and sisters as if they were physically related to us? How could that change the face of the church as we know it?

Day 60

Today's Scripture Reading: Matthew 13:3-9 and 18-23

DEVOTIONAL

From what you can tell about your experience sowing the seed of Christ, where has your seed fallen? It can be easy to get discouraged if our aim is always hitting the thorn patch, but it's important that you just keep on sowing. In this parable, Christ identifies four different types of landscape. He doesn't warn us that we shouldn't throw to the thorn-filled area because it will be a waste of our time and seed. To be honest, it's not up to us. We're only called to sow and sow generously. If one seed takes root in good ground, it will be worth all the times we got shut out, shot down, and denied by unreceptive ears and hearts.

Day 61

Today's Scripture Reading: Matthew 13:10-13

DEVOTIONAL

Teachers are genuinely challenged in today's classrooms because they have to try to teach in a manner that will engage ALL the students in their classroom, even though each student might learn in a slightly different manner from the others. Some learn by reading, and others by doing. Some are visual learners and others are audio learners. The teacher has to employ a number of different strategies in order to successfully get his or her message across to the students. In a sense, this is what Jesus was doing. If Jesus had simply spoken the Word bluntly, it would have resulted in mass confusion and minimal learning. Not a brilliant idea. Instead, he melded scriptural concepts into practical stories that would apply to the everyday lives of the people in His audience. The result? A connection! Your task today is to choose one parable that Jesus told and remake it using modern day terms and situations. Doing so may increase your understanding of this particular lesson or improve your ability to teach others and relate with them accordingly.

Day 62

DEVOTIONAL

Nowhere in these short stories do we see the main character mourning over what he had lost. He sold *everything* in order to gain a much greater treasure. It's unlikely that he hesitated while making the sale, pausing to think, "Oh, man. But I'm seriously gonna miss that!" But that's what we do sometimes, isn't it? We want to follow God fully and give it all over to Him, but sometimes we get caught up on the idea of what we have to give up instead of focusing on what we have to gain. Maybe you've thought, "I want to follow you, God, but I don't want to give up my friends. I don't want people to dislike me because they think I'm a fanatic." Or maybe you don't want to give up a habit, or your time, or money. What is one thing to which you are still clinging tightly? Attempt to let it go and focus on rejoicing fully in the spoils of the *true* treasure--your salvation and future eternity with Christ our Lord.

Day 63

Today's Scripture Reading: Matthew 14:22-24 and Mark 1:35

<u>DEVOTIONAL</u>

If you've ever read the Gospel books all the way through, you'll note that Jesus being surrounded by large crowds is a prominently reoccurring theme. Even when He's not with masses of people, His disciples are almost always right by His side. Peace, quiet, and privacy were a seriously scarce resource during His ministry. However, despite all that Jesus had going on, He *made* time to go off alone and spend time in prayer with the Father. Our lives are *so* busy and *so* over-scheduled these days. Does God have a reserved spot in your schedule, or do you simply try to pencil Him on a last-minute basis. You may have to turn down an invitation from time to time, and you may have to tell your spouse, "I love you, sweetheart, but I just need some me and God time right now." Mark a time slot in your schedule right now and commit to spending that time alone with God in prayer. It's refreshing; it's rejuvenating; and it's what Jesus did, so it's probably a pretty good idea.

Day 64

Today's Scripture Reading: Matthew 14:24-33

DEVOTIONAL

It's easy to be hard on Peter and judge him for being distracted in the midst of a miracle. It does seem ridiculous that even as he was walking on water, he saw the storm and was afraid. For goodness sake! He just saw Jesus calm the storm six chapters ago! But we certainly should respect Peter for getting out the boat. Jesus called him to do something, and he listened. It would have been easy for Peter to feign not hearing Jesus. Between the winds, waves, screaming disciples, and thunder, no one would have blamed Peter for shouting a giant, "WHAT?!" in Jesus' direction. Peter knew what Jesus wanted him to do, and he sincerely tried to summon all the faith he could muster in order to accomplish that calling. What is Jesus calling you to do in your life? If you know what it is, maybe you're afraid of failure. If that's the case, remember the story of Peter and that trying, trusting, and failing is better than never trying at all, just as long as Jesus is there to pick you up when you start falling.

Day 65

Today's Scripture Reading: Matthew 15:1-20

DEVOTIONAL

You've probably met some people who call themselves Christians, but only respond to certain verses in the Bible while explaining away the more challenging ones. They walk the walk of a Christian when it's convenient to do so. In this passage, Jesus speaks pointedly and powerfully about the dangers of treating traditions more highly than God's Word. Here, it sounds like the Pharisees were inconvenienced by a certain commandment, so they reasoned their way out of having to obey it. Tsk, tsk, tsk. Hopefully you're not blatantly disobeying a commandment of God, but there might be a tradition in your life that you're treating with undue respect. Consider if your reason for doing certain things or acting a certain way is rooted in scripture or habit.

Day 66

Today's Scripture Reading: Matthew 14:13-21 and 15:32-39

DEVOTIONAL

The disciples were ready to scold these tagalongs of Jesus. What are the odds that a population the size of a small city would all convene together and NO ONE would pack a sack lunch except for a little boy? Slim. Yet again, Jesus has the opportunity to provide for the needs of others, but the miracle in this instance is simple. He feeds them. Now, it is rather impressive that he feeds MANY with little, but the actual act of generously providing food for those who are hungry and in need is actually not that complicated. You may not be able to give sight to the blind or make the lame walk, but you can note that many in this world are hungry, and you can do something about it. How will you nourish someone today? You can make a difference in the life of at least one hungry soul whether you make a sandwich for the homeless man you pass every day on your way to work or make a donation to a "feed the world" charity or local food bank.

Day 67

Today's Scripture Reading: Matthew 16:5-12

DEVOTIONAL

It doesn't take the disciples long to forget what Jesus has done to tear down obstacles in their lives. Sometimes, it doesn't take us too long to forget, either! We laud and magnify His name when He answers a prayer or blesses us with a new opportunity, but then the instant we're faced with a struggle or roadblock, we panic! Think about the top three things that God has done for you that have truly helped you through a tough time and share those with your spouse. Sincerely try to commit those few things to memory so that tomorrow (or later today) when unexpected issues pop up, you can quickly bring to mind how wondrous Christ is instead of panicking unnecessarily.

Day 68

Today's Scripture Reading: Matthew 18:21-35

DEVOTIONAL

The fact of the matter is that there is not a single person on this planet who has sinned against you more than you have sinned against God. If you want to start keeping score as you play "The Blame Game," stop and think how you would place in those rankings. Is it harder or easier to forgive your spouse as compared to other people in your life? Discuss why this is the case and talk about why forgiveness is such an important part of everyday life. Big Hint: Verse 35 provides a pretty life-changing point of view on the whole concept of forgiveness!

Day 69

Today's Scripture Reading: Matthew 21:18-22 and Matthew 17:20

DEVOTIONAL

Some people don't take Christ's words in this passage literally. They assume that He's speaking in exaggerated terms for a grand effect, but Jesus is usually pretty straight-forward. In a nutshell, He says, "Believe and it will happen." The message is simple, but it is often us who complicates it. We attach "ifs" and "buts" and stammer and stutter because our faith is not unashamedly whole. What is the one thing you would want to accomplish if you could have the faith that Jesus refers to in these verses? Pray every day for the next week that the Spirit would work in you and see what He will do with your mustard seed-sized faith!

Day 70

DEVOTIONAL

Have you ever worked a job for under-the-table cash and not reported your earnings to the Internal Revenue Service? Maybe there's other sketchy/less-than-legit loopholes you've used in filing taxes that didn't give you guilt that kept you up at night, but you knew were not necessarily totally honest. Jesus says right here that we are to pay the necessary taxes to the government. It may require you to rethink your spending and record-keeping habits at times, but the right thing to do isn't always the easy thing. In fact, most of the time it isn't. It might not seem fair, and it might not seem glamorous, but to accurately report your taxes is to follow the teaching of Christ. Remember this around April 15th.

Day 71

Today's Scripture Reading: Matthew 22:34-40

DEVOTIONAL

If you had to choose only one passage to sum up the entire Bible, this one would certainly be a top contender. These two commandments sound so simple, but can be a daily struggle. Today, let's focus on verse 37 specifically. It's probably a verse that you have heard quite often, and maybe you've become numb to the revolutionary meaning it holds. Discuss the following questions with your spouse: What does it mean to love the Lord your God with all your *mind*? What might that look like in practice? What is the difference between loving God with all of your soul and with all your heart?

Day 72

Today's Scripture Reading: Matthew 24:36-44

DEVOTIONAL

What an exciting, but terrifying notion that Christ could come right...NOW! I hope that you're ready for the mysterious moment in which He will triumphantly return, and I hope that you are eagerly awaiting. In this passage, Christ mentions that we'll all just be going about our daily business when people will just start disappearing. One here, two there--but some people will be left behind. If Christ were to come *this very instant*, who would you wish you would have shared the gospel with sooner? Make a pact that you will find that person tomorrow and take the first step toward helping the Lord save their soul.

Day 73

Today's Scripture Reading: Matthew 25:14-30

DEVOTIONAL

The parable of the talents uses the idea of money management to illustrate a point, but in this context, "talents" can also be taken literally. Meaning this: God doesn't want you to be afraid and sit on your monetary blessings when you could be turning a profit on them. Likewise, he has entrusted each of us with actual talents that range from musical abilities to duck-hunting skills. In the same way, the He expects us to steward our financial blessings, He also desires that we will develop our talents and use them to the best of our ability. Discuss what each of you believes are your greatest talents and brainstorm how you could be using those talents to glorify the Lord.

Day 74

Today's Scripture Reading: Matthew 25:31-46

DEVOTIONAL

This is a well-known set of verses within the church. When we go out of our way to help someone in need we can be quick to pat ourselves on the back, check an invisible box off our mental checklist, and think, "Whelp! Helped that guy. Jesus would be proud." How often do we take inventory of all the people we came into contact with and *didn't* help? Or how about the ones that we don't even notice to being with? Each time you turn your back on the need of another human being, it's exactly like turning your back on Christ. What kind of plans and precautions do you and your spouse need to put into place to enable you to be more free in your helpfulness? Maybe you could leave the house earlier than you think you need to so you can open doors for others, give directions, and assist stranded drivers when needed. Or perhaps you could keep some fast food gift cards on hand for the times that you come across a man or woman begging for food.

Day 75

Today's Scripture Reading: Matthew 26:6-13

DEVOTIONAL

What is something in your life that has tremendously high sentimental value to you, but an exponentially different monetary value? It's interesting that some inexpensive things can hold the highest place of grandeur in our houses and hearts, but then other things that are ridiculously expensive may not actually mean anything to you at all. Sometimes it's not just about the value; it's about the *worth*. Jesus tries to clue the disciples in on this concept. You can't blame them too much for being dense here. There really were just trying to be good stewards in their finances. They missed the true message, though, however good-intentioned they may have been. When placing value on things, people, actions, and motives remember to look past the dollar sign and try to get a glimpse into the heart. You may just find an entirely different set of riches there unlike anything you've ever imagined.

Day 76

Today's Scripture Reading: Matthew 26:31-35 and 69-75

DEVOTIONAL

Here, we find yet another case where 21st century Christians totally call Peter out on his betrayal. "How could he possibly change his colors so quickly? A few short hours ago he was pledging his undying allegiance to Jesus, and suddenly he's turning his back on the man he spent the past several years of his life with?" In Peter's defense consider these two thoughts:

1.) You never know how you're going to react in a situation until you're actually in it, and

2.) Never underestimate the power of an accusing and slightly angry mob.

In this passage, Peter denies Christ by blatantly saying, "I don't know this man," when people inquired about his history with Jesus. It's unlikely that you've blatantly denied Christ by what you have said in the past, but is it possible that you have ever denied Him based on what you did *NOT* say? Sometimes there are opportunities to speak up for His holy name and we stand by saying nothing. If you can think of a time in which you have done this, then you probably already know that your silence betrays your allegiance in the same way that words against Him would.

Day 77

Today's Scripture Reading: Matthew 28:16-20

DEVOTIONAL

The death scenes are always some of the most dramatic and climatic parts of the movies, aren't they? As the movie character gets ready to pass on, he or she whispers out their last message for the remaining characters and that message is always so life-changing. Think about it--if someone close to you were dying, you'd treasure their last sentence forever. If it were an admonition, you would work diligently in memory of that loved one. Well, Christ doesn't die in this passage, but He does *leave* for an indefinitely long period of time. He could have said so many things, but what he chose to say was a straight-forward command to the disciples, us, and everyone who may come after us. "Go, therefore, and make disciples of all the nations, baptizing them in the name of the Father and of the Son and of the Holy Spirit (vs. 19, NIV)." Are you honoring Christ's last wishes? Maybe you need to talk with your spouse about participating in a mission trip to another country, or maybe you need to plant seeds in the fertile grounds of your own hometown. Discuss how you can make disciples of the world and commit to giving honor to these epic last words of our Savior.

Day 78

Today's Scripture Reading: Acts 4:13-22, 29-31

DEVOTIONAL

When the hot shots and big wigs of the town confronted Peter and John and told them they could no longer speak the name of Jesus, Peter and John reacted in an admirable way. They didn't succumb to political correctness and pipe down. They didn't become belligerent and argue, turning away people with their harsh answers. No, they simply stated the truth essentially saying, "How can we *not* speak about Him? We're compelled. We simply must pass this news along." It's like in Luke 19:37-40 when Jesus said that the rocks would cry out if the people somehow managed to silence their praises to Him. The message of Christ MUST be spread, and His praises MUST be made known. Do you feel like you're going to spontaneously combust if you don't leak the Good News of Christ's redeeming love to all those around you? If your answer is yes, then do something! Write a social media post, call a friend, or go make some spiritual small talk with a stranger. Don't hold it in any longer! If your answer is no, then ask yourself what it will take to become on fire for God again?

Day 79

Today's Scripture Reading: Romans 5:1-5

DEVOTIONAL

Many Christians have never actually been persecuted. Living in a country with the freedom to choose whatever religion you like, it's not a terribly common issue at this point in time. While it is a blessing to avoid persecution, it also leaves a potential gap in our spiritual development. Paul states in these verses that suffering can lead to a host of other godly characteristics. Persecution is only one way to develop these attributes, though. What are some other ways that you have experienced growth in perseverance, character, and hope in your life? How would persecution further your spiritual maturity if you were to experience it in the near future?

Day 80

Today's Scripture Reading: Romans 6:1-23

DEVOTIONAL

As we've discussed before, this whole concept of grace was a new thing for the Christians of Bible times. Like a child testing the boundaries of its parents, the Romans were trying to see just exactly how much sin they could get away with before reaching their allotted limit of grace and forgiveness. Paul was trying to tell them that they should want to turn from sin *completely* and not dabble in it any longer. Do you ever find yourself testing the boundaries of God's grace in modern times? Going along with the child analogy, we should try to please our heavenly Father just as we strive to make our earthly parents proud. Although earthly parents occasionally dole out consequences for negative actions, the worst consequence of all is their disappointment in you and your behavior. Imagine how much worse God's disappointment would be by comparison!

Day 81

DEVOTIONAL

This is a tongue twister chapter! Paul's message gets a little complicated in his wishy-washy manner of speaking, but he actually gives a pretty good description of the internal war that each and every one of us experiences on an ongoing basis. It's a battle between our conscious (what we know we should do) and our desires (what we want to do). It's all about our knowledge of Scriptures (again, what we know we *should* do) and fighting the impulses of this world (temptations, peer pressure, gut reactions/our sinful nature). It's exhausting, to say the least! What is something with which you have been battling lately? Something you know you should be doing differently, but just can't seem to make yourself submit to doing. Share this with your spouse and pray that each of you has the discipline to do the right thing going forward.

Day 82

Today's Scripture Reading: Romans 8:26-39

DEVOTIONAL

Have you ever had a word that was just on the tip of
your tongue? In your heart, you knew what you were
trying to say, but the words just wouldn't come out
quite, right? It always feels so good when someone
comes along and suggests just the word you were
trying to bring to mind. It's a definite "Ah ha!"
moment. Well, in a roundabout way, that is kind of
how the Spirit works within us. Our hearts murmur
out feelings and desires, and we just don't quite know
how to express them. It could be a potentially
frustrating situation, but it's ok because the Holy
Spirit speaks the lost language of our hearts! If that
doesn't make you feel special all over, I don't know
what would! Just imagine how in sync your marriage
would be if your spouse could interpret those inner
murmurings that even you didn't know how to
translate!

Day 83

Today's Scripture Reading: Romans 12:1-2

DEVOTIONAL

Offering your body as a living sacrifice is a simple enough concept for the believer. It means to dedicate your life to His will and to live in a manner befitting the name of Christ. By doing this, you will automatically take care of the first part of verse 2— not conforming to the pattern of this world. The tricky part comes in the second part of verse 2. What does it mean to "be transformed by the renewing of your mind (NIV)?" What do you need to be doing on a daily basis in order to ensure that this transformation takes place? Also, how will being transformed within the mind enable you to test and approve God's will for you?

Day 84

Today's Scripture Reading: 1 Corinthians 1:10-17

DEVOTIONAL

It's awesome when you can feel a sense of pride about the congregation you attend and a sense of unity with your fellow believers. However, it's easy to pit congregation against congregation and forget that we are *all* on the same team, working toward the same goal, and waiting for the same Messiah to return. Maybe you're saying, "Well, we have a better children's ministry than that church over there," or, "Our Vacation Bible School is really so much better." Or maybe you or someone you know has been a preacher-follower in the past--going wherever your pulpit minister goes and leaving congregations in your dust. Being a Christian isn't about choosing sides as far as which specific congregation to endorse or which preacher to listen to. The only sides that matter are whether you're playing for Jesus or for Satan. How do you think you can encourage teamwork and a togetherness that crosses congregational boundaries and why might this be important for our culture?

Day 85

*Today's Scripture Reading: 1 Corinthians 1:18-25
and 3:18-20*

<u>DEVOTIONAL</u>

If you hold firmly to the teachings of the Bible, it is guaranteed that the world will call you foolish. Scientists and philosophers will cry out for "proof" and condemn anything you throw at them to be "unscientific." The world holds these people up on a pedestal as wise and knowledgeable, but the Lords puts to shame the "wisdom" of this world. They will call your beliefs foolish, and you might not want to hear that, but you should take heart if you do. That means you're doing the right thing. In times like these, it's *right* when you're considered *wrong* by society. Have you ever been called out by someone in society trying to prove you wrong about the cross of Christ? If someone called you foolish today, what would your argument to that person be?

Day 86

Today's Scripture Reading: 1 Corinthians 1:26-31

DEVOTIONAL

Only in the Bible would we see a scrawny shepherd boy beating a giant and a grandma-aged woman giving birth despite decades of barrenness. Only in the Bible would an army of 300 men beat an enemy whose numbers could not even be counted. In this wonderful book a Christian-slayer becomes the most well-known Biblical author of all time, an insecure, stuttering man leads a whole people away from Pharaoh's armies, and a carpenter becomes King of all. The Bible is FULL of stories of the underdogs. What are the areas of your life in which you feel weak? Embrace these and pray that God will use you and your weakness in ways you can't even begin to imagine.

Day 87

Today's Scripture Reading: 1 Corinthians 2:1-5

DEVOTIONAL

Sharing your beliefs with strangers, or even people you know, can be an extraordinarily nerve-racking ordeal. It's easy to keep putting it off, all the while convincing yourself that you need to study the Scriptures more or perfect your pitch. We read in this passage that Paul didn't come to the Corinthians with a terribly eloquent presentation of the gospel. He was nervous, and his words weren't honestly anything special at all. The one notable thing about his message was this: it was *God's* message. If God really wants an individual to hear Him speaking to his or her heart, your measly lips will do the trick quite nicely. Do you struggle with overcoming the fear to share your faith? Have a practice conversation with your spouse right now and close your devo for today with a prayer to our Lord asking that He use your lips, trembling or not, to speak to others the words they most need to hear.

Day 88

Today's Scripture Reading: 1 Corinthians 3:5-17

<u>DEVOTIONAL</u>

It's only natural to want to see the effects of your efforts. If you spend all day mowing the lawn, you want to take one minute at the end of all the raking, weed-eating, and cutting to admire your handiwork. If you clean the whole house, you'd like all sticky hands, muddy feet, and shedding pets to chill for just a moment so you can bask in the sparkly grandeur of your dwelling. When it comes to the work of the Lord, though, you may never see the end result till we meet in heaven. Maybe you've planted multiple seeds in the lives of people you know and may *never* see those individuals come to Christ. It can be frustrating, but remember that God knows all things and will reward you according. Just think of how excited you will be when you see those "seeds" in heaven! In your life, who has planted a seed in your life that might not have been present to see the full effects of his or her efforts? If that person is still alive, call, text, or write an old-fashioned letter telling how his or her work made a difference in your life.

Day 89

Today's Scripture Reading: 1 Corinthians 5:1-13

DEVOTIONAL

Hot button topic, here we come. Some Christians believe that we shouldn't judge others, but Paul calls us in these verses to monitor the public sins of our fellow believers. To outsiders, the church might seem like a place where people who have it all together come to look down on others. That's certainly not the case. Christians have their issues and struggle with sin the same as everyone else. It's important that people know this, but it's also important that the church not endorse a blatant disregard for God's laws to become associated with the church's reputation. It's an uncomfortable topic to broach sometimes, but it might help to seek guidance from the elders at your church if there's a specific situation in your congregation that comes to mind or a particular question you have. Don't be afraid to search the Scriptures further if you still feel unsettled about the answer you receive.

Day 90

Today's Scripture Reading: 1 Corinthians 6:12

DEVOTIONAL

Jesus' death and resurrection entirely changed the rules for the Jews. They were used to following a super specific and burdensome set of rules and then-- boom!--they were introduced to this concept of grace and no longer had to adhere to the law of Moses. Their lives were turned upside-down, to say the least. All the sudden, this group of people had some phenomenal freedom! They didn't always know how to use it properly, though. What are some things that come to mind when you think of things that you are technically allowed to do, but that might not be the best thing for your spiritual walk and for your future? Do you think it's best to stay on the "safe side" of grace or to experience all things, so long as the activities are not directly prohibited in Scripture?

Day 91

Today's Scripture Reading: 1 Corinthians 6:15-20

DEVOTIONAL

Temples are not so common in Western civilization today, but we still have a vague idea of their purposes from reading history and the Bible. Temples were these oftentimes great buildings that were devoted to worshipping God. Everything about their presence pointed toward the Holy One and the bricks, candlesticks, people inside, and whole essence of the place were dedicated to God. It's amusing to think of our bodies in that manner. Perhaps you remember the story in Matthew 21:12-13 when Jesus erupted in anger because profit-hungry men were making the temple into a den of thieves. If Jesus got *so* angry due to that improper use of the temple, how do you think he would feel about your body being used to be intimate with anyone other than your spouse? Go one step further in this scenario and consider that your thoughts stem forth from your brain, which is also part of your body and is, therefore, a temple of the Holy Spirit. What changes do you need to make in *your temple* so that the Holy Spirit will feel completely at home there?

Day 92

Today's Scripture Reading: 1 Corinthians 7:1-9

DEVOTIONAL

If Paul is a role model to you, it can be difficult to hear him continually warn against the institution of marriage and hold up his own bachelor-style life as the preferred choice. Fear not, though. If you're married right now (and you probably are, considering that these devos are for newlyweds), you have made the right choice for you personally. Now that you *are* married, you may be either pleased, shocked, or interested to know that you no longer have "authority" over your body. This means that, in order to please the Lord, your husband, and ward off Satan's interference in your marriage, you ought to engage in intimate relations with your husband or wife as often as he or she desires. The great thing about this is that it works both ways! Although it may take some getting used to, this is a foolproof way to starve out sexual temptation and hurtful rejection in your marriage. Discuss the pros and cons of this view toward sexual intimacy and let your spouse know if you have any concerns about integrating the concept found in this passage into your marriage bed.

Day 93

Today's Scripture Reading: 1 Corinthians 7:10-16

DEVOTIONAL

Maybe within your marriage right now one of you is a
believer while the other one is still on the fence about
this whole "Savior" thing. Even if you are both
believers, there could be a time when your spouse
goes through a period of doubt or experiences such
heartbreaking loss that he or she turns away from
God. You should never *ever* give up on your spouse.
Making household decisions and raising kids with an
unbelieving spouse can be a tumultuous experience,
but you may be able to guide your spouse back to
Christ though your unwavering faith, actions, and
dedication to the Lord. If this is not a struggle
between you and your spouse right now, try to think
of one of your friends or brothers or sisters at church
who is currently dealing with this issue in his or her
marriage. Write that person a note or find him and her
and give a hug, prayer, and bit of encouragement.

Day 94

DEVOTIONAL

Here again, Paul talks about how single men and women can focus much more easily on working to please the Lord without being distracted by working to please his or her spouse. You can't seriously argue with that. What you may have to do is work twice as hard to ensure that you're putting Christ first, just like you did before you were wed. Let's take this time to be truly open and honest. Do you think your relationship with God has changed since you met and married your current spouse? If so, how? I would venture to say that it has most certainly changed, but if you work hard and constantly consider the challenges that lay before you, you can actually make that change for the *better* instead of for the worse. Talk with your spouse about how each of you can strengthen your relationship with God and try to predict what marriage-related items might try to get in the way of achieving that goal.

Day 95

Today's Scripture Reading: 1 Corinthians 8:1-13 and 10:23-33

DEVOTIONAL

Can't remember the last time I was walking through the meat section of the supermarket and saw a clearance sign stating, "Meat Sacrificed to Idols" on it. It's just not a modern day issue in this country anymore. The problem of inadvertently causing fellow brothers and sisters in Christ to stumble, however, is still quite relevant. The actual issues at hand may take the form of different stumbling blocks (drinking alcohol, watching certain actors or television shows, so on and so forth) but we still have fellow Christians with weak consciences within our brotherhood who we need to consider when making daily decisions. What are some stumbling blocks for you and how does it affect your faith when you see other mature Christians absolutely ignoring those stumbling blocks? Are there any blocks in your life right now that you might be ignoring which you know are bothering others in your congregation? Talk those situations through with your spouse and see if an alternative course of action is needed.

Day 96

Today's Scripture Reading: 1 Corinthians 9:19-23

DEVOTIONAL

Paul was a chameleon of sorts in his mission work. If he could relate with a group of people, he did! It was that simple. He didn't share the good news with only his next door neighbors or just the people who grew up in similar circumstances to his own, but instead he preached to every person he could reach. He stayed true what he was deep down inside (a Christian) but pulled on past experiences in order to start meaningful conversations with those who needed to be saved. What kind of past experiences can you use as you strive to make disciples of those with whom you come into contact? You're married, for one, which means that you can easily have at least one thing in common with other couples. Maybe you were an athlete in school or perhaps now you have a specific hobby or career that opens a door with a certain population of people. Use *all* those unique things about you to further the message of Christ and become all things to all men.

Day 97

Today's Scripture Reading: 1 Corinthians 9:24-27

<u>DEVOTIONAL</u>

If you or anyone you know has ever run a marathon, you know that training is an absolute *must* for such a race. You don't just strut up to the start line and wing it. You must subject your body to WEEKS of training (or torture, in the eyes of non-runners), and you've really got to dedicate yourself to the goal of finishing the race. Our Christian journey certainly shares some parallels with that sort of training. Christian training must be regular, challenging (meaning you delve deeper and deeper into the Bible much like you try to run longer and faster each time as you train for the race), and there must be an end goal. For a race, it's enough to finish and maybe you get excited if you beat your own personal time. Best case scenario: you win by running faster than everyone else and get an earthly prize. The race we run has a far, *far* greater reward waiting for us at the end. So, where are you right now in your training? What steps do you, as a couple, need to take in order to move your performance up to the next level?

Day 98

Today's Scripture Reading: 1 Corinthians 10:1-13

DEVOTIONAL

Sometimes it's easy to assume that we would have exponentially stronger faith than we do right now if only we had been present to experience some of the miracles that took place in the Bible. If only we could have physically sat at the feet of Jesus, listening to his parables and learning from his many teachings. If only. Here's the thing, though---those people who experienced the Bible in real time sinned just like we do today. They did incredible things, but they also experienced some pretty epic failures. We do have one tool that they would have desperately wanted, though. We have the Bible. Whole, complete, and readily available in multiple languages, versions, sizes, and colors. We are meant to read this wonderful historical account and learn from the mistakes of those who came before us. That's just what we're going to focus on doing for the next several weeks. We're going to look at some key characters in the Bible and see what lessons we can glean from the triumphs they yielded as well as from the mistakes they made. In doing so, we will follow Paul's admonition faithfully.

Day 99

Today's Scripture Reading: Genesis 2:1-24

DEVOTIONAL

The first couple in all of history actually acted in a strikingly similar manner as couples in today's day and age. They were swayed by worldly deception to disregard the Lord's instruction, they thought they could hide their shameful actions from God, and they played the blame game. They didn't exactly get the world off to a great start, did they? The world's first newlyweds were deceived. That deception is still going on today but in a wide variety of different ways. It's interesting that Adam tried to blame Eve for this poor decision, even though he was there, as well. God ends up punishing both of them, thus illustrating that couples are teams and will oftentimes be treated as such. Consider this as you make decisions on behalf of your spouse. The repercussions may reach more widely than you anticipate.

Day 100

Today's Scripture Reading: Genesis 3:1-16

DEVOTIONAL

Here, we see a firsthand example of some *serious* envy/anger management issues. Abel gave the <u>best</u> portions from the <u>firstborn</u> of his flock. Cain, on the other hand, gave God "an offering." Cain didn't necessarily give God a *bad* offering, but he didn't give Him the best and it is implied that he gave Him leftovers. Cain's anger was misplaced because of his envy toward his brother. While he should have been disappointed with himself for skimping God, he instead became angry at his brother for making him look bad. THEN he thought he could hide the truth from God. He made mistake, after mistake, after mistake in this situation and God punished him for it. Has there ever been a time when you chose to be envious of another person rather than improve your own circumstances? Blaming others for your own stunted growth can damage relationships and set you down a dangerous path. Discuss how you can avoid that path in the future.

Day 101

Today's Scripture Reading: Genesis 6:1-22

DEVOTIONAL

Noah is the absolute ideal example of ignoring peer pressure. The ENTIRE WORLD was evil. So evil that God felt the need to call out, "Redo!" Can you imagine how much sin there would have been in those times? But in the midst of all that calamity and pure evil, there was Noah. Noah, the man who walked with God, just doing his own thing. There's an awful lot of sin going on today. Would history books identify you as a couple that "walks with God" or one that follows the crowd? What does walking with God even look like and why does it become increasingly important as sin gets more and more prevalent in our world?

Day 102

Today's Scripture Reading: Excerpts from Genesis chapters 12, 16, 20, 21, 25, and 26

DEVOTIONAL

Isaac, in so many ways, was just like his father. The Lord spoke to both Abraham and Isaac, promising a vast land and offspring that would be innumerable in Genesis 12:1-9 and Genesis 26:1-6. Both of their wives were initially barren, but God granted children to them because of their prayers (Genesis 16:1, Genesis 21:1-7, and Genesis 25:20-21). Abraham and Isaac both married beautiful women who they feared would be the death of them, so they fibbed to powerful men saying that their wives were, instead, their sisters (Genesis 12:10-20, Genesis 20:1-18, and Genesis 26:7-14). Interesting how parallel their lives turned out to be. In what ways are you like *your* parents? Take this time to get to know a little more about your mate and his or her family history.

Day 103

DEVOTIONAL

This short exert out of Abraham's life teaches us the simple concept of family love and sharing. Abraham inherits the land of Canaan from God in Genesis chapter 13, but tensions rise between Lot's herdsmen and Abraham's herdsmen. You don't hear Abraham pipe up and say, "Well, Lot, maybe you should pray to God that He blesses *you* with some land. This patch is mine!" He behaves quite differently than that! He not only gives Lot half of the land, but he allows Lot to choose which half he wants. And then when Lot gets captured and robbed, his faithful uncle Abraham rides in to the rescue. This type of selfless love seems rare, in Bible times as well as today. What is one thing you can do for a member of your family today (brother, sister, uncle, aunt, niece, nephew, cousin, or all of the above) to show some modern-day selfless love?

Day 104

Today's Scripture Reading: Genesis 19:1-26

DEVOTIONAL

A simple one verse sentence is dedicated to the demise of Lot's wife. Brief as it is, we can learn from her (literally) grave mistake. Sodom was a terrible place brimming with depravity and sin. Lot's wife had to sit by as her husband offered her virgin daughters to be essentially raped by the prowling townsmen. Though they didn't take Lot up on his offer, even the idea of it must have been difficult for his wife to handle. I find it unlikely that she *liked* Sodom, yet she cast a glance back at it, fearful to leave the one place she knew as home. Unfortunately, she had disobeyed a direct command, and it was the last thing she ever did. Your past life wallowing in sin--that's like Sodom. It's evil, banished, and you should avoid any backwards glance you might be tempted to take at it. So look forward into God's bright future for you and leave those sins and burdens behind!

Day 105

Today's Scripture Reading: Genesis 25:22-34, 27:1-45, 32:1-33:15

DEVOTIONAL

If ever anyone had a reason to maintain a grudge against his brother, it was probably Esau. Jacob was power hungry from the start, even in his mother's womb. He took advantage of Esau's desperate hunger and used it as bargaining power and THEN he tricked his dad into giving him a blessing that was never seriously intended for him. He was deceptive, manipulative, and persistent. When he came face to face with his brother after many years of separation, he had every right to be shaking in his boots. Esau, however, had forgiven his brother and moved on with his life. If Esau can forgive Jacob for absolutely derailing the direction of his future, surely you can forgive whoever has wronged you, either recently or in the past. When Esau moved past his anger, he was able to marry, start a family, and truly enjoy life. Release a grudge that you've been holding on to and enjoy the refreshing feeling of contentedness as it washes over you.

Day 106

Today's Scripture Reading: Genesis 29:1-30:24

DEVOTIONAL

The relationship between Rachel and Leah was probably like the relationship between many siblings around the world--competitive! You wouldn't believe the one-up-manship in this family! They each cried out to God saying, "This isn't fair!" The crazy thing is that God actually listened to their complaints and tried to level the playing field between them. Noting Jacob's lack of love for Leah, He decided to bless her with LOTS of sons (the highest honor in that culture at that point in time). Then, seeing Rachel's displeasure for so many years, He decided to open her womb and bless her with a son, as well. Two pretty basic lessons we can learn from this rivalry are 1.) Life will never truly be fair and 2.) If you are diligent in offering your prayers up to God, He might attempt to make life a little more "fair." Just remember next time you're wishing you had something that someone else has that you probably have something they want, as well. We're all blessed differently and "fairness" is a pretty much a fantasy.

Day 107

Today's Scripture Reading: Genesis 39:1-23

DEVOTIONAL

Considering this passage, I would say that it's safe to call Joseph "The Man with a Plan." Potiphar's wife was probably attractive, and she was certainly persistent. It would have been easy for Joseph to fall into sin with all that was working against him in that situation. He was able to resist that temptation because he made a conscious decision that he would not offend God and his employer in that manner. With that resolution in mind, he was able to rely on his gut instinct of running when Potiphar's wife attempted to seduce him. Had he not recognized the potential peril ahead of time, his gut instinct might have been quite different. We can see that Joseph's main mistake was allowing himself to be alone with Potiphar's wife. Is there a member of the opposite sex who you are spending an extended amount of time alone with (on a required or voluntary basis)? Husbands and wives, is there someone of the opposite sex who is showing an abnormal or inappropriate amount of interest in you right now? Even if there is not, do you have a *plan of escape*, should it ever happen?

Day 108

Today's Scripture Reading: Today's Scripture Reading: Exodus 3:1-4:17

DEVOTIONAL

Moses was like many of us--enslaved by the concepts of what he *was not* capable of doing instead of focusing and what he *was* able to do. You would think that having God tell you that you can do something would be all the pep talk you could ever need, but Moses continued to argue with God about his abilities. We can learn two different things about Moses from this brief period of his life:

1.) Don't argue with God. If He has a plan for you, you're probably going to end up carrying that plan out anyway, so you might as well do so willingly.

2.) *If you do argue*, God might just give you a teammate. God told Moses that Aaron could speak to Pharaoh, and this gave Moses the boost of confidence he needed to get the job done. You know what's most appealing about that whole situation? Moses is recorded in Scripture as speaking to Pharaoh almost as often as Aaron is. Sometimes we just need someone by our side to give us the courage to do what we know in our hearts we are meant to do. As you go through your marriage, your spouse might be your Aaron--a capable teammate, but mostly just someone to encourage you, so you never have to stand alone again.

Day 109

Today's Scripture Reading: Numbers 12:1-16

DEVOTIONAL

It's easy (especially with family) to fall prey to the green-eyed monster of jealousy. In this passage, we see that Moses' siblings, Miriam and Aaron, were talking bad about Moses behind his back. They judged his choice of bride and were envious of his elevated status when they perceived that they were equally important in leading God's people out of Israel. The lesson that we can learn from this story is that there is *always* someone listening. If you're bad-mouthing someone else, they person you are talking about could be right around the corner. Or maybe someone else might overhear you and relay the message to him or her. Even if none of that happens, Gods hears everything you say (and knows everything you think, for that matter). To speak against a servant of His is a terrible thing to do. Avoid causing such dissention within the brotherhood at all costs.

Day 110

*Today's Scripture Reading: Deuteronomy 34:9-12
and Joshua 1:1-9*

DEVOTIONAL

Have you ever taken a promotion at work and worried
that maybe you wouldn't be able to fill the shoes of
the person who held the job before you? Imagine how
Joshua felt when he had to step up after Moses' death
and led the Israelites into the Promised Land? The
Bible even goes so far as to say that there was
NEVER another prophet like Moses, who spoke to
the Lord face to face (Deut. 34:10). Talk about a
tough act to follow! But Joshua didn't get cold feet.
He didn't compare himself and find that he fell short.
All he had to do was listen to his own personal pep
talk from God ("Be strong and courageous....I will be
with you..." Joshua 1:5-9) and he was able to cross
the Jordan River and destroy the city of Jericho by
walking a few laps. All this goes to show us that it's
not the capability of the person, but the power of God
that matters most.

Day 111

Today's Scripture Reading: Joshua 2:1-24 and Joshua 6:21-25

DEVOTIONAL

We learn from the story of Rahab that help can come from the most unlikely of places. It was less-than-ideal to have spent the night in the house of a prostitute, but this "harlot" was a key piece in God's plan, just as much as Moses and Joshua were. If you can remember choosing teams in P.E. when you were in middle school, it was usually the same story. The most athletic and popular students were chosen first, and the less popular, slower, scrawnier students were left for last pick time and time again. You will encounter people in your daily comings and goings who have spent their *entire lives being picked last.* Never underestimate the worth and potential power of a supposed "second class citizen." God has a plan for that person just the same as He has one for you.

Day 112

DEVOTIONAL

The story of Samson strongly (pardon the pun) illustrates the power of a beautiful woman over a man as well as the power of persistence. I have always wondered why Samson told Delilah the true secret to his strength. He knew she was leaking information to his enemies. He knew this because she'd tested his trick answers time and time again. But still, even he grew tired of her persistent pestering and succumbed to honesty (which cost him dearly) in the end. You might consider this story the next time someone in your life is badgering you to join in with a sinful activity or turn away from something you know is right. You may be able to resist them for a time, but you may need to call in the reinforcements (perhaps alerting your spouse to help you defend against that pestering) in order to endure for the long haul.

Day 113

DEVOTIONAL

Gideon certainly is an interesting and particularly doubting Biblical character. Even though he was visited by an Angel of God, he still needed some help with his faith. God spoke directly to him saying, "...save Israel from the hand of the Midianites. Have I not sent you (Judges 6:14)?" Seems to me the Lord saying, "Go" should be prompting enough, but not for dear, old Gideon. Even after receiving his pecking orders he *still* requires not one, not two, but THREE direct signs from the Lord in order to gather up the courage to fight the Midianites. He led Israel to a triumphant victory, though, and against all odds! 300 men versus an innumerable army. We can learn that God's power can be clearly seen, even with a doubtful man leading the way. If you feel God calling you to do something but aren't convinced it's Him or that you're hearing the message clearly, go ahead and take the first step forward. A half-willing mind is better than feet that won't move at all.

Day 114

Today's Scripture Reading: Ruth 1:1-Ruth 4:22

DEVOTIONAL

From Ruth, we learn that fierce loyalty can go a long way. Even when it made complete sense for her to abandon Naomi, even as Naomi was *begging* her to do so, Ruth would not leave her mother-in-law's side. Ruth's reputation in town was the she was a virtuous woman, and she gained the favor of Boaz based on the care she showed her mother-in-law. The most important thing to remember in this story is that which is not directly addressed. We hear of Naomi's grief (changing her name from "Pleasant" to "Bitter"), but we do not know what Ruth was going through. Ruth's husband had died, and she was likely mourning and lost, but she persevered. Ruth is a shining example of hope in a desperate situation. The next time you feel down and don't think you can go on any longer, remember Ruth and her gumption. It might just be for you as it was for her and a bright new future could be waiting around the corner.

Day 114

Today's Scripture Reading: 1 Samuel 17:1-50

DEVOTIONAL

One of most well-known stories in the Bible is that of David slaying Goliath. What can we learn from this dear biblical hero?

*David knew who he was. In verses 38-39, Saul is trying to beef little Danny boy up and make him into a fierce warrior. But that's not who David is. He's a shepherd, and he didn't feel the need to put on airs, trying to trick the Philistines into thinking he was something else entirely.

*David had confidence in God. He speaks with faith and assurance in verse 46. Do you feel confident with the skills and tools that God has provided you, just as David was confident with his slingshot and unlikely status as a warrior?

*David knew where he needed to be. In verse 28, David's brother scolds him for leaving the sheep. In what way would God's will have been fulfilled if David had stayed with the flock? It's easy to get accustomed to your daily grind and overlook the needs that come your way. If you keep your eyes open, though, God might just put a Goliath in your path so that you can show His power to everyone around you.

Day 115

Today's Scripture Reading: 1 Samuel 19:1-20:42

DEVOTIONAL

David and Jonathon were like peanut butter and jelly---so good together. These guys were best friends through thick and thin, and they actually did endure some pretty thin times. Maybe you've had a friend your parents weren't crazy about in high school, but have you ever been BFF with someone your parents wanted to *kill?* Jonathon had to navigate those rough waters, and I can imagine that it was quite unpleasant and tense in that household. But you can learn something from the friendship that David and Jonathon had. It was a solid relationship built on mutual admiration, trust, and dedication to one another. You have the opportunity to enjoy this covenant type of friendship with your spouse for the rest of your lives! Embrace it!

Day 116

Today's Scripture Reading: 2 Samuel 11:1-27

DEVOTIONAL

The day before last we learned that David was able to please God by leaving his post and going where he wasn't "supposed" to be. Something marvellous happened then, but such is not the case in this particular story. David was supposed to be at war, but instead he found himself staring at a naked woman, who just so happened to be married to one of his soldiers. It can seem so odd that David was able to triumph over a GIANT, but not a woman. One reason for this is because in the first story, God was on David's side. The second reason is because you should never underestimate the power of a beautiful woman. To the wives: consider the power your body possesses. Harness that power by being modest at all times and only giving your husband the privilege of seeing certain aspects of your physical beauty.

Day 117

Today's Scripture Reading: 2 Samuel 12:1-15

DEVOTIONAL

In this passage, Nathan had to be the bearer of bad news/enlightenment and correction to David. As a Christian spouse, you may be called to serve in this manner more often than you might like. Note the way that Nathan handled this situation. He didn't come right out and tell David, "Woah, man! You are totally sinning!" He worked his way into that message by forcing David to relate to his situation in a more objective way. While either way may work, you should consider the best way to approach your spouse when you perceive that he or she is blatantly sinning against God. Like David, he or she may simply be blind to the reality of the situation.

Day 118

Today's Scripture Reading: 2 Kings 2:1-11

DEVOTIONAL

How cool would it be to forego the regular getting old and dying thing and *instead* be taken up to heaven in a chariot of fire? Talk about going out with a bang! Elijah allowed God to do many fantastic things through him (causing a long drought and then the subsequent rain, providing the widow with endless bread-making materials, bringing the widow's son back to life, standing up to Baal's prophets, etc.), but his exit from this world is one that certainly leaves an impression. Elijah knew he was about to be taken and he asked Elisha, "What can I do for you before I leave?" Seems a little counter-intuitive from what our culture believes. If you were dying, you would probably ask others to do things *for you*. But what if your last wish was to bless others and help THEM, instead of focusing on you and what you might be leaving behind? It would be the ultimate selfless act. We will all leave this earth at some point in time, and most of us won't have the privilege of exiting in a chariot of fire. When it's your time to go, what will your last wishes say to others about you? If you don't already have a will, consider having one drawn up. As you ponder what to put in your will, ask how you can bless others as your final act of selflessness.

Day 119

Today's Scripture Reading: Esther 2:19-23 and 6:1-12

DEVOTIONAL

There are many reasons why Mordecai is an awesome example and many things we can learn from him, but today we'll just focus on my favorite Mordecai-related lesson. **You should always do the right thing, even if no one recognizes you for it.** Mordecai saved the king's life and didn't even get a pat on the back (Esther 2:19-23). But he didn't do it because he would be rewarded; he did it because it was the *right thing to do*. It just so happens that things ended well for him when the truth came to light (Esther 6:1-12). Sometimes you'll get recognized for your good deeds, and sometimes you won't--Don't let recognition change your intentions.

Day 120

Today's Scripture Reading: Esther 2:8-15 and 4:6-17

DEVOTIONAL

The actions and example of Esther can teach us a little bit about decision-making. First of all, when Esther was competing (for lack of a better word) to become queen, she accepted wise counsel from those who were more knowledgeable about the royal conditions than she was. Second, although she resisted at first, she knew how to make a hard decision when it came to letting God use her in His master plan. Going before the King could have meant her death, but she heeded her uncle when he said, "You won't be safe in the palace. You can chose to turn the other way, but God will save the Jews somehow. You can be a part of His plan or not. Your choice (Paraphrase of Esther 4:13-14)." Most hard decisions can boil down to that basic decision---help God carry out His will or not. What's it gonna be?

Day 121

Today's Scripture Reading: Job 1:1-2:13

DEVOTIONAL

Oh, Job. There is so much we can learn from you. On the bright side, you experienced sheer torture for 42 chapters and did not give up. On the other hand, you, unfortunately, chose to surround yourself with an unsupportive network of friends. Job's wife was a particularly unsupportive individual, as we see in Job 2:9 when she tells Job to "curse God and die." Harsh. His friends insisted that Job must have sinned, causing God to punish him, and should therefore repent. It is likely that you have avoided trials that match the extremes of Job's trials, but you have surely endured some hard times in your life. What kind of difference has the support of your spouse, family, and friends made in the past? What can your spouse do in the future to support you when you are struggling?

Day 122

Today's Scripture Reading: Job 38:1-40:5

DEVOTIONAL

Job's second mistake was his constant questioning of God and His overall plan and knowledge. After Job mourns, mopes, and challenges God for several dozen chapters, God finally answers Job (albeit sarcastically). It's not necessarily wrong to question God from time to time. He knows that we will experiences times of doubt. We should, however, listen for His answer. Job did the smartest thing in Job 40:5—he shuts up. An extraordinary thing happens when we ask and then listen. Sometimes God will answer! Is there anything that you have you been asking God about lately, but that you have not given Him a chance to answer? Take a moment to pray together now. Assure God that you know He can see the big picture, that you are willing to wait for an answer and that you will listen for His response going forward from here.

Day 123

DEVOTIONAL

Despite the handful of David's downfalls that Scripture records, he has been and will forever be known as "a man after God's own heart." What an honor! It is such an encouragement that we are able to see the times that David has excelled and the times that he has failed. This helps to reassure us that we can still be in God's favor and in pursuit of His heart despite the hiccups we might experience in our journey to becoming the best Christians we can be. In honor of David being a man after God's own heart, spend today trying to be like him by doing the one thing for which he was most well-known. No...not slaying a giant or participating in an adulterous relationship—writing a psalm! Read one of his many examples in the book of Psalms if you need inspiration and then write a brief praise to our Heavenly Father. Also, feel free to share your psalm with your spouse once you're done!

Day 124

Today's Scripture Reading: Daniel 1:1-16

<u>DEVOTIONAL</u>

As we see in this reading, our friend Daniel was into eating organic before it was even cool. We can take a couple lessons away from his clean-eating. 1.) If you truly want to be healthy, strong, and make the most of the body God gave you---eat your veggies and cut out the calorie-rich drinks! 2.) (And more importantly,) don't submit to peer pressure. We use the word "peer pressure" when we talk about middle-schoolers, but we don't admit that societal pressures don't just fade away once you graduate high school or college. The world is *always* going to have this predominant or "popular" lifestyle that tempts you to conform without thinking about the consequences. Think! Just because everyone else is doing something does not mean that it is the best or right thing to do in God's eyes. Don't be afraid to stand out because you're doing things differently. What is something you've been doing in your life that is purely based off of what everyone else does? Discuss an alternative to that lifestyle and see if you can consider a better way. And, as with all things, make sure whatever you're doing is in step with the Bible.

Day 125

Today's Scripture Reading: Daniel 3:1-30

DEVOTIONAL

Some people say that the story of Shadrach, Meshach, and Abed-Nego is one of absolute fearlessness. However, perhaps it wasn't fearlessness as much as it was integrity that they displayed. The scriptures do not indicate as to whether or not the men were afraid; it simply states that they made up their mind about the matter and stood their ground. In verse 17, they say that they have a God who is *able* to deliver them from the furnace. They don't say that He WILL save them, just that He is able to do so. But the question of whether or not God would spare their lives wasn't important to them. The only thing that mattered in those life-altering, decision-making moments was whether or not they would deny God. In a moment of true terror, we might think that death is the worst punishment. We forget that, as Christians, death has no grip on us! How might this realization change your life and way of thinking going forward?

Day 126

Today's Scripture Reading: Jonah 1:1-4:11

DEVOTIONAL

The main thing we can learn from Jonah is that it's useless to run when God has a mission in mind for us. Whether or not we say it out loud, there are probably some people who we don't think deserve to hear the gospel of Christ. Or maybe we think they should hear it, but that it would be a waste of our time to present it. Three words for you on that topic: Not. Our. Call. We don't get to pick and choose who the most worthy recipients of the Good News are because God intends for EVERYONE to hear it. No exceptions! What is a neglected population that comes to mind who you believe should receive a chance for redemption? Prostitutes? Inmates? Join a prison ministry (or start one!) and get involved with a nonprofit that caters to desperate women. Who knows? God might just use to you to change hundreds or thousands of lives.

Day 127

Today's Scripture Reading: 1 Corinthians 11:2-16

DEVOTIONAL

This can be a controversial chapter of the Bible that we might be tempted to skip over, but there's a valuable message here that wives and husbands need to know. The issue of whether or not a woman is to cover her head during prayer is an intriguing one, but Paul ultimately leaves it up to us when he says, "Judge for yourselves," in verse 13. What you need to know is that while man and woman are equal, there is a hierarchy involved. The husband is *always* to be the head of the woman, just as the head of man is Christ and the head of Christ is God. There is no shame in this; only an opportunity for wives to bring glory to their King *and* to their husbands. Wives, how can you show the world that your husband is the head of you? What changes do you need to make within your marriage (and with your attitude) to reflect the truth we find in this passage?

Day 128

Today's Scripture Reading: 1 Corinthians 11:17-34

DEVOTIONAL

The Lord's Supper in Biblical times was much different from how we carry it out today. There was no baby nibble of crackers and mini-shot glass of grape juice. The Lord's Supper was oftentimes a literal *meal*. In this passage, Paul reprimands those who were pigging out at the meal with the prime intent of filling their bellies, as opposed to the actually intended purpose of remembering Christ's sacrifice and sharing in that memory through fellowship with the other brothers and sisters within the church. We bring shame to the Lord's Supper when we quickly bite and pass, drink and pass without taking a moment of reflection to consider all that Christ has done for us and what His sacrifice means to us today. The Lord's Supper is not simply a task that we check off our to-do list; it's a privilege! Discuss at least three different ideas you could put into action that would you help you focus your minds during the Lord's Supper and practice those tactics this coming Sunday.

Day 129

Today's Scripture Reading: 1 Corinthians 12:1-27

<u>DEVOTIONAL</u>

We tend to overvalue the talents, skills, and gifts that other people have while tragically undervaluing our own. What a shame. Even thousands of years ago this was an issue in the church! Everyone wanted to have the more prominent spiritual gifts, assuming that if they had those gifts they would be a better Christians, more helpful to the church, and more spiritual in God's eyes. Wrong! God created *all* gifts and He created them in such a way that they would work together beautifully, like a ballroom waltz or like the final pieces in a complicated puzzle. Homework time! Each of you should get out a piece of paper and make two columns. In the first column, write down what you believe your spiritual gifts (or really any talents/skills that you might have) are and write down what you believe your spouse's spiritual gifts are in the other column. For each column, write down at least three items. When you're finished, share your answers and brainstorm how each of you can use those talents to glorify God.

Day 130

Today's Scripture Reading: 1 Corinthians 13:1-3

DEVOTIONAL

The old adage, "It's the thought that counts," is really quite true in this instance. Paul is eloquently saying that you can know all there is to know, have the most impressive spiritual gifts and faith known to man, and give every bit of yourself to a cause, but if you don't have love it's almost as if you did nothing at all. It's harsh but so true. If you've ever gotten someone a baby shower gift or birthday present just because you felt obligated to do so, then you know that there's no real feeling behind that act of generosity (other than maybe resentment). We, as Christ's disciples, *must* do everything out of love, or our efforts are all for naught. When well-intentioned activities and projects are spurred on by something other than love, do you think the community can tell? How does it affect the general public's impression of Christians as a whole and of the work we do?

Day 130

DEVOTIONAL

When it comes to marriage, this may be the most frequently quoted Bible passage of all time. Perhaps you even had this Scripture read aloud at your wedding ceremony. Paul offers a concise definition of what love *is* and what love *is not* in these verses. Thinking strictly about your relationship with your spouse, which of these do you feel that you excel in exhibiting? Which do you struggle with the most? Write this passage on a small notecard and put it on your car dashboard or bathroom mirror so that you'll be sure to see it every day. As this week progresses, remember which characteristic of love you struggle with the most and make an effort to work on it over the next several days. Each time you see the notecard shoot up a short prayer to God asking that He aid your efforts to be a better husband or wife.

Day 131

DEVOTIONAL

Have you ever wondered why God allows painful
experiences to plague us? Some tunnels look as
though they have no light at the end and we might be
tempted to think that no good can come from those
bleak situations. Paul tells us that suffering allows us
to connect with others and comfort them in a
meaningful way. Think about it. If you've ever been
struggling with a big heartache (loss of a family
member, issues of infertility, etc.), some of the most
practical and life-changing advice comes from those
who have endured such a situation themselves. What
kind of suffering have you and your spouse
experienced in the past? What comfort helped you
most and who do you think the Lord is calling you to
comfort now?

Day 132

Today's Scripture Reading: 2 Corinthians 2:3-11

DEVOTIONAL

In earlier messages from Paul, we have been told that it's important to confront a brother or sister who is blatantly sinning within the church. Here, we see that the Corinthians did just that, but they took it one step too far. They confronted the sinner but did not reaffirm their love for him or her. Paul reveals that Satan can genuinely use that kind of division as the perfect foothold to sneak into the church and spread his schemes. As he says in verse 11, we are not always aware of Satan's schemes, but what are some ways that you've seen Satan try to pull apart churches in the past?

Day 133

Today's Scripture Reading: 2 Corinthians 3:1-3

DEVOTIONAL

Paul oftentimes uses such beautiful imagery in his letters. We see that the Corinthians act as Paul's letter of recommendation, which leads us to consider the fact that our lives also read like a letter to those who know nothing about our God or about Christianity as a whole. Have you ever sensed that the letter-version of you was being read? If someone were to symbolically "read" your heart today, what is the message that they would find? Write down in one page or less the content you believe that person would find and share your letter with your spouse.

Day 134

Today's Scripture Reading: 2 Corinthians 4:7

DEVOTIONAL

Do you ever have days when you just feel totally and utterly plain? Maybe you feel like a small fish in a big sea or like there's nothing particularly special about you, but you couldn't be more wrong! You have treasure inside of you; the light and message from God that He is the one true God and His love endures forever. God *can* speak through fancy, famous people, but much of the time throughout history, and even now, His message can be heard most powerfully from a lowly soul who doesn't have much to brag about. Can you feel this treasure within you? Go out and share it with someone!

Day 135

Today's Scripture Reading: 2 Corinthians 4:16-18

DEVOTIONAL

Day after day after day you may begin to notice that your joints creak when you get out of bed in the morning. Maybe you're having to spend a few extra minutes in front of mirror plucking out those gray hairs or analyzing those "life lines" that seem to have appeared on your face overnight. There's no doubt about it---our physically bodies are only temporary loans, and we will notice the changes as we get closer and closer to that expiration date. Don't worry, though. Even as you note your body slowly aging, be encouraged that your inner self is forever young and renewed daily! Should there ever come a time when you are struggling to see past your aging physical self, I would encourage you to write these verses (and verse 16, especially!) on a notecard and affix that friendly, heavenly reminder to your bathroom mirror.

Day 135

DEVOTIONAL

In verses 2 and 4 of this passage, Paul mentions groaning. We oftentimes associate that word with discomfort, but Paul means it in this reading to mean "longing." Do you find that you are *longing* to be clothed with your heavenly being? Are you tired of this earthly lifestyle and ready to say hello to eternity in heaven? I hope that your answer is a resounding "Yes," but suspect that you may sometimes struggle with being attached to this world. There's nothing wrong with wanting to have kids someday or to see your current kids have grandkids. It's a glorious thing to experience life, but our true yearning should be to experience heaven above all else. Are we getting too comfy down here in this temporary home of ours? Unite in prayer with your spouse right now and ask that God would light the fire of desire within your heart that burns for *heaven* and ask that He help you keep your priorities in line as the world tempts you with all that it has to offer.

Day 136

Today's Scripture Reading: 2 Corinthians 6:11-18

DEVOTIONAL

People should be able to look at us (as Christians) and see that we are different. We shouldn't blend in with all the nonbelievers of this world, and we shouldn't have our closest relationships be with non-spiritual people. Now, Paul isn't saying that you shouldn't associate with non-believers at all. Of course not! If you didn't interact with the world at all then you would never be able to save anyone in it. He *is* saying that you won't have the most important things in life in common with a non-Christian, so that might complicate your relationship. Additionally, the world might confuse YOU for a nonbeliever if that's the crowd you surround yourself with on a daily basis. Who are your closest friends and confidants? Are they believers or not? How does this affect your relationship with those friends?

Day 137

In a story like the one when the woman gave her last two mites, we see overwhelming generosity flow from the Macedonians. Paul didn't even ask them to give (since they were *so* financially strapped), but they insisted on doing so! Paul is trying to get the Corinthians to see three things in this chapter. 1.) It's all about attitude when it comes to giving; 2.) If you're in a tight spot, you may receive blessings from God's people in order to keep you afloat; and 3.) You should give according to what you have and not what you *do not* have. The tithe is a good starting point for giving, but it's an Old Testament concept. In the New Testament, we're told to give in consideration of *all* that we have. Where is your giving today? Are you sticking steady at about 10%? Could you make some room in your budget to give more?

Day 138

Today's Scripture Reading: 2 Corinthians 9:7

DEVOTIONAL

Whatever you do decide to give, you should give it cheerfully. This verse implies that you should choose that amount ahead of time and not just toss in whatever cash you have on you when the collection plate is passed. If you commit to giving a certain amount to God, that means that some weeks you might have to go without something else. Should your spirit ever become negative or unwilling, you may need to take a step back and evaluate your reasons for giving. It you're only giving because you feel that it is expected of you, that is not a good reason. God is really hoping that you will *want* to give. When you have a desire for helping others, it makes parting with your money practically inconsequential. When you're struggling with such negative thoughts, it may help to remember the following things: a.) It's not your money. It always has been and always will be God's, and b.) When is a time that giving has felt rewarding to you? Think back on that instance and imagine how you can repeat that feeling over and over again if you can manage to give with a cheerful heart.

Day 139

Today's Scripture Reading: 2 Corinthians 10:7-18

DEVOTIONAL

It's essential to have some self-worth and to feel good about what you're doing for the Lord, but you need to steer clear of boasting about yourself and the work that you're doing. It's kind of like fishing for compliments. Does a complement mean more when it comes from someone randomly, sincerely, and with no prior coaxing or hinting or when you've perfectly set yourself up to receive one? When the Lord commends you, *that* will be your reward. Any measly boastful words that you or anyone else could have said about you will seem flat, and of little importance once you hear what the Lord has to say. Have you ever met anyone who was quick to boast about the things he or she was accomplishing? What kind of impression did that person make on you?

Day 140

Today's Scripture Reading: 2 Corinthians 11:13-15 and that Matthew 7:15-23

DEVOTIONAL

False teachers can take on all different forms, but more often than not they probably seem like pretty good people who are teaching a message they truly believe in. However, just because they believe what they are teaching and just because what they're teaching *seems* good doesn't make it right. 2 Corinthians 11:15 says that Satan can work through people who appear to be doing righteous work. He probably thinks that no one will suspect them, but we should look at any variance on the gospel suspiciously because Jesus tells us himself in Matthew to look out for false teachers. What are some messages that are circulating right now that you believe fall under the category of "false teachings?"

Day 141

Today's Scripture Reading: 2 Corinthians 11:24-33

DEVOTIONAL

It is difficult to make a case for complaining about our struggles as Christians after reading this passage. It's amazing that God preserved Paul's life through all those struggles, and it's also amazing that Paul was able to maintain his sanity and zeal. But Paul is only a man---a flawed human being just like us. If God were calling you to endure such trials, do you think that you would be able to stay true to Him through it all? Consider that question the next time you find yourself throwing a mini pity party when your faith makes life a little more complicated for you.

Day 142

DEVOTIONAL

Many scholars have spent untold hours and energy trying to figure out exactly what Paul's "thorn in the flesh" was. While we might be curious, that knowledge wouldn't change the meaning of this passage one bit. I believe that Paul was trying to tell us two things, in particular. 1.) Sometimes we ask, and ask, and ask, and God still says no. 2.) Your weaknesses allow Christ the chance to show His strength. Society today tells us to show no weakness. When asked what our weaknesses are in a job interview, we're encouraged to put a spin on a strength like, "I work/care too much." I'm not telling you to air all your struggles on your first day at a new job, but I do think we need to stop wearing these perfect facades that fool others into thinking we've got it all together all the time. Think of one weakness you've been struggling with right now and ask someone (other than your spouse) to pray for your ability to handle that situation.

Day 143

DEVOTIONAL

The knowledge that you are a son or daughter of Christ has the power to turn around any bad day. There's simply no better news than that! We're not the only ones, though. All who have been baptized into Christ are His sons and daughters, too, and we're all *equal*. Are you treating all these fellow brothers and sisters equally? We have a tendency to pick out our friends at church or to identify with the other people who talk and dress like us or who are our age and fit our demographics. Sometimes this leaves some populations falling between the cracks---not very "equal" at all. Next time you go to church, I challenge you to try and find someone who looks out of place and maybe like a bit of a wall flower. Pull him or her into your group and make that person feel like a true brother or sister.

Day 144

Today's Scripture Reading: Galatians 5:1-6

DEVOTIONAL

In Paul's day, it was extremely difficult for new Christians to turn their backs on the Jewish law they had been upholding their whole lives. It was all they knew, and the idea of liberty was not only liberating, but terrifying! Even the Gentiles seemed to want to impress more laws upon themselves than they genuinely needed to. We do that sometimes, too. It's hard to live life right, so we make black and white rules to guide us along, ignoring the greys and scooting toward legalism even though Christ freed us from the burden of the Old Law. How do you think legalism complicates Christian living? Are there areas of your Christian walk where you tend to want to impose old rules and regulations in?

Day 145

Today's Scripture Reading: Galatians 5:19-26

DEVOTIONAL

Paul gives a pretty clear description in this passage of what a Christian does and does not look like and how we ought to act. The fruit of the Spirit is comprised of nine seemingly-simple characteristics that we should spend out whole lives trying to obtain, maintain, and nurture. Which fruit of the spirit seems to come to you naturally? Which one (or ones) do you find yourself struggling with more often than not? What about your spouse? Have an open discussion and you may find that each of you excels in different fruits. As you both seek to nourish these characteristics in your daily lives, you can help each other and encourage one another along the way.

Day 146

Today's Scripture Reading: Galatians 6:1-2

DEVOTIONAL

As you move forward in your spiritual journey, you will undoubtedly see fellow Christians fall off the bandwagon. As they travel down less-than-Christian paths, you shouldn't be afraid to reach out to them and offer some guidance and encouragement. They may be offended, and they might keep right on going down that sinful path, but that doesn't mean you shouldn't try to persuade them to repent and remind them why they chose Christ in the first place. After all, wouldn't you want a brother or sister in Christ to reach out to you if you were straying? Paul does offer this admonition; be careful, lest you become tempted by the thing you're warning that person against. Satan can use your good intentions for evil if you let him. Have you ever known a friend who was trying to "save" others, but ended up becoming lost in the process? If so, how might this have been avoided?

Day 147

DEVOTIONAL

Do good. In a world that is full of so much hate and pain, loneliness and loss--do good. It may seem like you're walking up a down escalator sometimes, but that doesn't mean you should stop doing good. As a matter of fact, that probably means you should step it up a notch! Paul says we should do good to all (and *especially* fellow Christians), as we have opportunity. Don't see any opportunities? Well, I'd say it's time to invent some! This week, do *at least* one random act of kindness for someone within your congregation and as well as one more for someone who is not a Christian.

Day 148

Today's Scripture Reading: Ephesians 2:1-10

DEVOTIONAL

Can you even imagine where you might be if it weren't for God's mercy? What your life would be like without grace? Sometimes we forget how powerless we are to save ourselves and get to thinking it's our *works* that open up the path to heaven and not pure and simple grace. Maybe it's because our faith is weak or maybe it's because we just think our actions hold more power than they actually do, but whatever the reason is, we need to stop thinking that we could go anywhere without grace. What does God's grace mean to you? If you had to describe it in three words, what would they be?

Day 149

Today's Scripture Reading: Ephesians 3:14-21

DEVOTIONAL

We bring our thoughts, cares, concerns, desires, dreams, ideas, and goals to God in prayer, but we sometimes forget how powerful He actually is. We oftentimes ask for specific, small, measurable things forgetting that God can do *immeasurably more than all we ask or imagine.* Let's start praying some God-sized prayers and having some God-sized dreams! Take the limits off your prayers and ask for God to blow your mind with the results. Substitute "you" and "your" for words like "us," "we," and "our" and pray these verses out loud with your spouse. The words are powerful, and the potential repercussions are even more so if you pray with a yearning heart.

Day 150

Today's Scripture Reading: Ephesians 4:26-32

DEVOTIONAL

Considering the fact that you are a newlywed couple, you have probably already been advised by several couples and marital enhancement books to adhere to this verse. It's a good rule to abide by. Don't go to bed angry. Even non-Christians know this concept (although they may not know that it's from the Bible). We tend to tune out after we read the verse about not letting the sun set on our anger, though. If you continue to read on, you'll find some suggestions on how you should "fight" while you're awake. Substitute slander and bitterness with compassion and forgiveness. If you were both to commit to handling anger in this manner, none of your arguments would last long at all! Choose one item from this list to work on improving in your "fight life" and discuss why it's essential not to go to sleep angry.

Day 151

Today's Scripture Reading: Ephesians 5:8-14

DEVOTIONAL

I find two things in particular interesting about this passage.

1.) Verse 10- Find out what pleases the Lord. Do you remember when you were first dating your (now) husband or wife? You probably made a concerted effort to learn your loved one's favorite color, foods, flower, sports teams, clothing brands, and so on and so forth. You wanted to please your mate, and you did your research to make sure you knew what he or she would like the best. Have you done that with God? Do you know what pleases Him and furthermore, *do you do it?*

2.) Verse 11- It's not good enough to just avoid the deeds of darkness--we are to EXPOSE THEM! Is it hard? Yes. Will it be uncomfortable to do? Almost certainly, but Paul is clear when he gives us our mission. When is the last time you "exposed" a deed of darkness?

Day 152

Today's Scripture Reading: Ephesians 5:22-33

DEVOTIONAL

Love and respect- that's pretty much all that marriage boils down to as it simmers and simmers over the years. Husbands, do you love your wives? Wives, do you respect your husbands? If your answer is yes, can your spouse *tell* that you love and/or respect him or her without you saying so with words? It is a beautiful thing that Paul compares the marital relationship to Christ's relationship with the church. We know that Christ loved the church in the ultimately sacrificial way; do we love our spouses in that way? If your answer was yes, can strangers on the street and people in your life tell that you do?

Day 153

Today's Scripture Reading: Ephesians 6:1-3

DEVOTIONAL

We tend to hear this verse as a child, and once we move out of the house we don't think it applies to us anymore. This concept of obeying and honoring parents is a lifelong one, though. What kind of relationship do you have with your parents and with your in-laws? Are you even interacting with them enough to practice this teaching? Being on your own and newly married is an exciting time and you can feel like you're big stuff at this point in your life. Just remember, your parents may have wisdom to offer if they have been happily married for decades. You can respect them by listening to their advice, honor them by asking for it, and love them as you invite them to be a part of this new phase of your life.

Day 154

Today's Scripture Reading: Ephesians 6:10-17

DEVOTIONAL

If you grew up in the church, you have probably heard about the armor of God from a young age. It's easy to become desensitized to such an incredible outfit of strengths. It's an amazing thought to think that these six weapons of offense and defense can protect us not only against the dark powers of this world, but also from spiritual forces outside of this physical world. In a battle of moral proportions, which item of armor is your go-to, number one choice? How can you improve your armor so that you'll be better prepared to conquer evil? Do you need to learn how to better yield the sword by memorizing and understanding more scripture or do you need to enforce your shield by praying for stronger faith? Whatever it may be, make that improvement a priority because you never know when Satan will attack.

Day 155

Today's Scripture Reading: Philippians 2:1-4

DEVOTIONAL

Paul speaks about being like-minded in this passage. I think he's referring mainly to the church body, but you might ask the same question regarding your marriage. Are you and your spouse like-minded regarding all the things that matter most? What would you say the main goal of your marriage is? If you don't have goals, you might want to take this time to talk about some potential ones right now. Paul indicates that being of one spirit and one mind comes naturally when each of you is putting the other person first, so just keep being selfless, and the unity of mind will come almost effortlessly.

Day 156

Today's Scripture Reading: Philippians 2:5-18

<u>DEVOTIONAL</u>

This is a tremendously powerful reading that almost always cuts to the heart. It's simply impossible to imagine being equal with God and having to endure all that Christ endured for us. It's no coincidence that Paul moves from speaking about Christ's sacrifice and the terrible experiences He overcame straight into talking about how we shouldn't complain or argue. The stark contrast certainly puts things in perspective. Christ, who deserved the best and got the ultimate worst, never complained, yet here we are grumbling about ridiculous first world problems like needing bigger houses to fit all of our possessions. Each time you feel yourself about to open your mouth to complain today, try to remember how Christ bore it all for us with no complaints and see if you can't swallow your words. The great thing that happens when you are able to do that is non-believers actually notice when you don't complain and start to wonder what is different in your life that makes you so happy and thankful for anything that comes your way!

Day 157

Today's Scripture Reading: Philippians 3:12-16

DEVOTIONAL

It's easy to esteem Paul as the best of the best. His New Testament words guide us through the treacherous waters of being an upright Christian in a crooked world. But Paul wasn't perfect. He said himself that he was always striving to attain his goal. What we can learn from him is this: You will try and you will fail. What you *must* do is move past the failures and try again. Sounds simple, right? More often than not the memories of our long-lost failures pop up when we least expect them, like when we're trying to do something new or when we're working to patch up a relationship. Give yourself a break and let the negative self-talk go. Paul did. Chances are that you were not a Christian-murderer earlier in your life, so if he can get over that, I think you can overcome your failures, too.

Day 158

Today's Scripture Reading: Philippians 4:4-7

DEVOTIONAL

Prayers can often be heavy on the requests and a little light on the rejoicing. Paul says that we should ALWAYS rejoice. We should be so thankful that everyone around us knows that we're blessed and proud of it! You may thank God for the big things in your life (your family, food, shelter, etc.), but how often do you thank Him for the small pleasures and treasures with which He blesses us? For example, when was the last time you rejoiced over having a flushing toilet, bones that don't break (you *could* have brittle-bone disease), or eyelashes that catch your sweat? Your challenge for today: Make a list of 100 random things about which you want to rejoice! Go ahead and pick the first items that come to your mind, no matter how simple, because God's blessings come in all different shapes, sizes, and variances of randomness.

Day 159

Today's Scripture Reading: Philippians 4:8-9

DEVOTIONAL

If you turn on the news for even a few minutes, you'll see that it's not super common for the world to dwell on noble, pure, and lovely things. Quite the contrary! The stories that circulate the most at work are the ones that awaken shock, fear, and judgment. As Christians, though, we are called to focus on the right and excellent things around us. The world is full of so much bad that it's easy to sometimes be fooled into thinking that's all there is. But God blesses us daily, and we just have to change our point of view (think "blessing-finding vision" as opposed to "rose-tinted glasses") and look for His hand. Right now, tell your spouse three things that have been concerning you. Then it will be the challenge of the spouse to see if he or she can identify the silver-lining in those situations.

Day 160

Today's Scripture Reading: Colossians 2:4-10

DEVOTIONAL

In this scenario, a tree serves as the perfect example of a believing Christian. No matter how tall, beautiful, fruitful, or magnificent one may appear at first glance, the true strength of a tree is hidden from sight. A strong root system, deep and intricate, is what all trees need to stand the test of time! As Christians, we are called to root ourselves in Christ, too. If we do this, when the wind howls and it sounds like smooth-talking arguments against the true gospel and deceptive ploys, we will stand firm and unmoved. Are you grounded in Christ today, with roots that burrow deep into the ground and receive nutrients and water (Scripture and unity with the Holy Spirit) on a daily basis?

Day 161

Today's Scripture Reading: Colossians 3:1-17

DEVOTIONAL

In order to "set your minds on things above" it may be helpful to know what setting your mind on things below looks like. It might manifest itself through constant and senseless worries. You might constantly compare yourself to others through social network sites or maybe you're always looking for the next best thing for your wardrobe, house, or kitchen in magazines, TV shows, and pinning/inspiration websites. If you were to estimate, what percentage of your time each day do you think you spend thinking about "things above?" Consider setting calendar reminders on your phone to alert you throughout the day that it's time to think of higher, nobler things. Make an effort to spend five solid minutes at the very start of your day thinking of such things.

Day 162

Today's Scripture Reading: Colossians 4:2-6

DEVOTIONAL

Two things to consider in this Scripture reading:

1.) Paul asks the Colossians to pray for him and to specifically request that God open doors for Paul so the message of Christ could be spread. Are you praying for the missionaries and preachers you know on a regular basis? If not, take some time right now to ask the Lord to open hearts and door for those individuals preaching the message.

2.) Paul also suggests that as we answer those who question us, we do so in *grace*. Tempers can flare when you're talking about a topic as important and sensitive as religion, so remember to be gentle, even if you know you're right. Many a well-meaning passionate Christian has been labeled a "Bible-beater" and avoided by some people simply because he or she forgot to season their conversations with grace.

Day 163

Today's Scripture Reading: 1 Thessalonians 5:12-22

DEVOTIONAL

This section is full of great calls to action that will enhance your marriage, church, and relationships with family, friends, and coworkers if you let it. I'm going to pluck out one particular verse and focus on it, though. Verse 12 tells us that we should acknowledge the hard-workers among us and those who care for us in the Lord. This could mean the elders in your church, perhaps a family member, or even someone you don't know directly, but whose work you have seen over the course of your time within your congregation. Brainstorm with your spouse and make a short list of the individuals who come to mind when you read this passage. Consider approaching these people with the next week and letting them know that you see their work, appreciate it, and are thankful to God for their care and sacrifice.

Day 164

Today's Scripture Reading: 2 Thessalonians 3:6-15

DEVOTIONAL

We're living in a society in which many avoid work like it's a plague. Generations pass down tricks of the trade on how to scrape by so that others will take care of the needs and wants of a lazier, select few. It's wrong. There may be government programs to support it, but we read right here that we are to avoid idleness, lest we starve. It is important to remember how Paul and his workers toiled endlessly so that they could provide for themselves while not placing a burden on others. Whenever it is possible, avoid taking the lazy way out; idleness offers a foothold to Satan and where laziness abounds, sin follows.

Day 165

Today's Scripture Reading: 1 Timothy 2:8-15

DEVOTIONAL

For the ladies: It's clear that you are called to be modest in your manner of dress. Paul spells it out right here, and also suggests that you look past the ornate adornments that call attention to such a worldly state of mind. Your good deeds should stand out more than the fancy, new necklace you're wearing, or the elaborate outfit you've been saving for a rainy day. I challenge you to go through your closet this week and analyze what your clothes are saying about you. Can your good deeds shine through or are your choices of apparel choking them out?

Day 166

Today's Scripture Reading: 1 Timothy 3:1-13

DEVOTIONAL

Men, even if you're not sure if you want to be a deacon or an elder in your church in the future, these characteristics are still not bad targets to aim for. Do the elders and deacons in your church provide upstanding examples of these descriptions for you? As you grow and mature as a man of Christ, which of these characteristics do you think you will need to dedicate the most time to perfecting? Women, consider this: Deacons and elders are required to have a wife and a household that is managed well. Are you a teammate/cheerleader as your husband works toward being eligible for this honorable position, or are you more of a stumbling block? Verse 11 is directed specifically to the women, so remember that even though elders and deacons must be men, the women in their lives play paramount roles, as well.

Day 167

Today's Scripture Reading: 1 Timothy 4:8-10

DEVOTIONAL

How much time do you spend working out at the gym each week? What percentage of your time is spent doing push-ups, swimming laps, pressing weights, and running miles? Paul says that physical training has *some* value, but GODLINESS is the true winner of the day. They're kind of similar, though, aren't they? Both require hard work, a shift in priorities, and in the same way that exercising promotes a longer, healthier life, godliness gives value to the lives we are living. If you are an avid work out fan, I would encourage you to spend your work outs pondering the eternal implications of living a godly life and how you might seek to exude such godliness in your daily walk.

Day 168

Today's Scripture Reading: 1 Timothy 6:6-10

DEVOTIONAL

The idea in verse 10 has oftentimes been misinterpreted from Scripture. Some in the world assume the fact that money *is* evil, when, in fact, Paul says it is the LOVE of money that can lead to all sorts of evil. He also says that we came into this world with nothing and we should be content to leave with nothing, as well. That can be a tough pill to swallow. If you were to lose everything today, would you be content, so long as your immediate needs were met? What items would you miss the most? Why are you so attached to those things and what can you do, going forward, to reduce your reliance on these temporary things?

Day 169

Today's Scripture Reading: 2 Timothy 3:1-5 and 4:1-5

DEVOTIONAL

Do these verses describe the current climate of our world, or what? It's a dead-on description, if you ask me! Verse 5 of chapter 4 describes what you need to do, though. People are a' sinnin' left and right. They hear the truth, but they will not listen. Instead, they'll make their own rules and live a life to please themselves, while absolving themselves of any guilt. So what do you do? You just keep preaching. They won't listen? You keep talking. And what if they punish you for your persistent ways and righteous message? 'Atta boy...keep up the good work.

Day 170

Today's Scripture Reading: Titus 2:1-8

DEVOTIONAL

It's interesting that this verse talks about how older women are to teach the younger women everything from how to run their houses to how to interact with their husbands. We kind of live in a "mind-your-own-business-I'll-run-my-house-how-I-see-fit" kind of world, but that sort of thinking does us a disservice. Are there older women in your family or congregation who have passed down valuable, biblical advice to you as you started your marriage and established your home? If so, make a concentrated effort to remember that advice and also to learn from any mistakes you make along the way. It may be helpful to keep a small journal on hand so that once you are in the position of being an older, wiser woman you can share that valuable information with a younger generation of wives and mothers later on.

Day 171

Today's Scripture Reading: Hebrews 4:12

DEVOTIONAL

We are exceptionally blessed to live during a period of time when we can enjoy the Bible so easily. Not only is it complete (as opposed to only having the Old Testament to refer to, as Paul, Peter, and all the other NT celebrities did), but we have complete access at all time. It would be easy to have a copy of the Bible in every room of your house, in both your cars, and on your desk at work. You can carry it everywhere with you in your phone, and you can also listen to audio recordings of it on MP3 players or on your computer. The Word of God is everywhere, but are we truly hearing its message? The writer of Hebrews indicates that we should be cut to the heart by the things we read in God's Word. When was the last time you were truly touched by something you read in Scripture and what kind of change did you make in your life as a consequence of that realization?

Day 172

DEVOTIONAL

This passage would have a whole different meaning for you if you had been an early Christian who had killed countless sacrifices in hopes that blood would erase your sins. Little did they know, it was only the blood of *one man* that had the power to wipe the slate clean for all mankind. As the writer of Hebrews was penning these words, there's no telling how many sacrifices had already been made. Picture football stadium after football stadium filled to the brim with the blood of useless sacrifices. Even after Christ died and was raised, some Christians had a hard time ceasing the sacrifices they had grown so accustomed to making. They were trying to work their way to heaven. Can you blame them? Many today are *still* trying to work their way to heaven but in different ways. What are some of the modern-day ways that Christians attempt to earn their salvation?

Day 173

DEVOTIONAL

This passage is yet another that brings to light something we typically take for granted. In Bible times, Jews were not permitted to go into certain parts of the temple. There were some places that only the High Priest could enter, and even he could only enter the holy of holies once a year! We don't deal with hierarchies like that---Jesus tore down those barriers when He died for ours sins. We can come directly to Him (with no need to be in a super special room or to ask a High Priest to intercede for us) and speak with Him on a one-on-one basis. How often are you taking advantage of the fact that you can confess directly to God, as verses 22-23 describe? No matter your answer, remember that you now have 24/7 open line to the Lord. Strive for a *constant* connection and you will sense unity with the Spirit like you have never known.

Day 174

DEVOTIONAL

Just after highlighting this amazing one-on-one, 24/7 relationship, we can have with our Lord and Savior in the verse prior, the write of Hebrews reminds us that we need to unite with our brothers and sisters in Christ, too. While coming together as a church congregation can unquestionably be encouraging for you as an individual, it's not the only reason to come to Sunday school and worship service. This passage indicates that coming together as a body can result in "love and good works" being stirred up and exhortations taking place. "Going to church," as many have come to coin the process of uniting as a group of believers, is actually more about others rather than yourself. Consider pondering what you can do for your fellow brothers and sisters on Sunday and Wednesday, instead of asking, "What can I get out of this service and how does this meet my needs?"

Day 175

Today's Scripture Reading: Hebrews 11:1-40

DEVOTIONAL

If you looked back through the branches of our Christian family tree, you'd see that faith is a HUGE part of our heritage. Over a dozen wonderful examples of faith are mentioned in this chapter, but not all of these individuals had *unwavering* faith. Many of the people in these stories are just like you---trying your hardest to believe, feeling Superman strong in your belief one day and super confused the next. In some ways, faith reminds me a lot of the sacrifice many men made during the Revolutionary War. Those men gave their lives because they believed in something bigger and better than themselves. They hoped for the freedom of America and gave up everything for something they would never see realized. The same is true for the examples in this chapter. They yearned for the new covenant and the promise of eternal life but died regardless. Do you have a faith that can sustain you through joy and trials, up and downs, for the rest of your life?

Day 176

Today's Scripture Reading: James 1:19-27

DEVOTIONAL

We can learn lots of great things from this passage, like to be sure to monitor our words, eliminate moral filth from our lives, and avoid anger. Basically, Paul is telling us that it's not enough to talk the talk; you've really got to walk the Christian walk. He concludes by saying that one way we can "walk the walk" is to care for orphans and widows. When is the last time you did that? Not everyone can handle foster care or inviting a childless-widow to stay in their guest room, but you can help in other ways. Volunteer to serve as a "Big Brother" or "Big Sisters" to parentless children. Offer widows you know rides to church and other community activities. Cook a meal with your spouse and bring it someone who needs it more than you. You can show your love for these forgotten populations in so many ways.

Day 177

Today's Scripture Reading: James 2:14-26

DEVOTIONAL

What good does it do to say to God, "I truly believe you have the power to do amazing things in my life," but to never step out on a limb or be willing to un-schedule your day in order to allow Him room to move about your life? Who are you actually helping if you tell the homeless man on the corner that you believe things will look up for him in his life, but you don't even entertain the idea of helping him find a job or get some warm food in his belly? We make a big deal out of faith and cry out about its importance, but won't move our hands and feet to do the *work* of faith in our life and the lives of those around us. Faith *is* important, but on its own is like a car with no wheels, a ship with no sail, and a train with no tracks---it's not going anywhere! How will you let your faith be evident in your works today?

Day 178

DEVOTIONAL

We can teach our pet dogs to speak and be quiet, yet we cannot control the words that come out of our mouths. It's one of the many ironies of life. The tongue may be the biggest dead-giveaway as to whether or not a person truly is a follower of Christ. Maybe you've heard someone assert, "I'm a Christian," one day and the next moment be spouting off gossip, cuss words, and complaint, after complaint, after complaint. Speaking in this manner drags the name "Christian" through the mud and results in God's followers being stereotyped in the worst possible way. There may be days when you are upset and impatient and simply can't think of anything nice to say about a situation. These are the days when you may need to realize that staying silent is a much better honor to the Lord than grumbling your discontentment, no matter how justified you feel in doing so.

Day 179

Today's Scripture Reading: James 4:13-17

DEVOTIONAL

You probably have some big plans for your life together, and that's great! You're newlyweds! Why shouldn't you? The changes that will occur within the next several years of your life are some of the biggest and most exciting of your entire existence. You might want to go back to school, change careers, buy a house, build a house, have a child, move to a new city, or participate in any slew of other activities. I would challenge you to verbally respect the will of God and *His* plan for you whenever you talk about these endeavors. It doesn't take much effort to tack on a, "if it's His will" on the end of a sentence. By doing so, you will send the message to believers and unbelievers alike that God is in control of your life and that you embrace that fact and are thankful for it.

Day 180

Today's Scripture Reading: 1 Peter 2:11-17

DEVOTIONAL

It is an interesting concept to think that we can minister to others and show our submission to the Lord by submitting to the government officials He has allowed to manage our country. Did you know that obeying the laws could preach Christian concepts to the world? Going the speed limit-check, score one for Christian living. Obeying building restrictions, water restrictions, and litter laws? Check, check, check. Who knew that not texting when you're driving could serve as the ideal example of honor to governing officials? In examples such as these, we can show bystanders that, although we are free, we live within the rules that have been set before us. It also gives others one less thing to use as ammunition when they attempt to drag the Christian name through the mud.

Day 181

Today's Scripture Reading: 1 Peter 5:8-9

DEVOTIONAL

Society has softened the image of Satan in many ways. Cartoons portray him as a mischievous, pitchfork-wielding busy-body who would like to mess up your plans whenever he gets the chance. Satan's not that simple, though. Life would be easier if he were. The devil doesn't want to mess up your plans, he wants to mess up YOUR LIFE. Causing your life to be uncomfortable or chaotic won't make him happy, though. He won't be satisfied until your soul is forfeited and your eternity in hell is set. He's sneaky, and he'll use whatever means possible to ensure that your devotion to God is only skin deep. A comfy life is *just* what he'd like you to have--feeling safe and secure when all the while he's camping in your living room. Don't underestimate his schemes. The war with him is not a game and, even if it were, you can't afford to lose. In what ways do you think Satan has been trying to creep into your life lately and how will you take a stand against his intrusion?

Made in the USA
Middletown, DE
27 September 2016